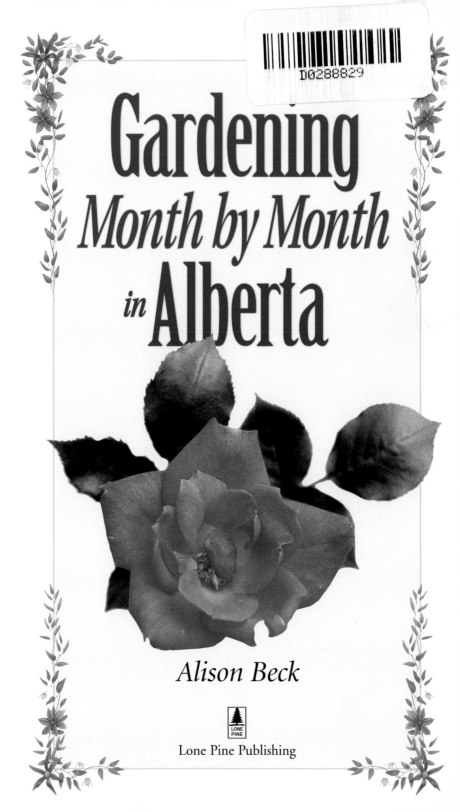

Gardening
Month by Month
in Alberta

Alison Beck

Lone Pine Publishing

The Publisher: Lone Pine Publishing

10145 – 81 Avenue
Edmonton, AB, Canada T6E 1W9
Website: www.lonepinepublishing.com

1808 B Street NW, Suite 140
Auburn, WA, USA 98001

National Library of Canada Cataloguing in Publication Data

Beck, Alison, 1971–
  Gardening month by month in Alberta /Alison Beck.

  ISBN 1-55105-143-5

  1. Gardening—Alberta. I. Title.
SB453.3.C2B44 2002   635'.097123   C2002-911252-4

Editorial Director: Nancy Foulds
Project Editor: Sandra Bit
Editorial: Sandra Bit, Lee Craig
Researchers: Don Williamson, Laura Peters, Carol Woo
Production Coordinator: Jennifer Fafard
Design & Layout: Heather Markham
Cover Design: Gerry Dotto
Production: Jeff Fedorkiw, Lana Anderson-Hale, Ian Dawe, Elliot Engley, Lynett McKell, Curtis Pillipow
Illustrations: Ian Sheldon
Photographers: Tamara Eder, Tim Matheson
Scanning, Separations & Film: Elite Lithographers Co.

Front cover photographs (L to R) by Tamara Eder, golden marguerite, forsythia, poppy, painted tongue, sweet potato vine; *by Tim Matheson*, daylily, dahlia, calendula.

The photographs in this book are reproduced with the generous permission of their copyright holders. *Additional photos:* **January:** Don Doucette (dogwood, juniper), EuroAmerican (coleus); **February:** Alison Penko (crabapple), Kim O'Leary (begonia), Elliot Engley (seed propagation), Heather Markham (tower planter); **March:** Dawn Loewen (forsythia), Linda Kershaw (dogwood), Joy Spurr (water garden); **April:** Peter Thomstone (foxglove), Heather Markham (spiral juniper), Robert Ritchie (climbing rose); **May:** Therese D'Monte (forget-me-nots); **June:** Heather Markham (containers on steps), Laura Peters (potted annuals); **July:** Horticolor© Nova-Photo-Graphik/Horticolor (cobaea); **August:** Colin Laroque (dahlias), All-American Selections (petunia), Peter Thomstone (evening primrose); **September:** Alison Penko (euonymous), Laura Peters (primrose), Erika Markham (birdfeeder), Don Williamson (birdfeeder), Laura Peters (bee balm); **October:** All-American Selections (pumpkins), Jen Fafard (carrots, assorted fall vegetables, gladiolus in buckets, tomato in hand, viburnum, ears of corn, plants on shelves, sunflowers in buckets), All-American Selections (cucumbers), Trevor Horbachewsky (grapes); **November:** Jen Fafard (hoarfrost on branches), Don Williamson (hoarfrost on trees), Anne Gordon (ornamental kale a), Joan de Grey (ornamental kale b), Janet Loughrey (ornamental kale c), Anne Gordon (ornamental kale, outside corner), Peter Thomstone (white iris), Dawn Loewen (magnolia), Heather Markham (azaleas); **December:** Saxon Holt (poinsettia cover and outside corner), Jen Fafard (peace lily, indoor water garden, braided bamboo, flower bouquets).

Frost date maps: adapted from the *Agroclimatic Atlas of Alberta* with permission from Alberta Agriculture, Food and Rural Development. *Climate normals and extremes charts:* adapted from the Meteorological Service of Canada, with permission from Environment Canada.

We acknowledge the financial support of the Government of Canada through the Book Publishing Industry Development Program (BPIDP) for our publishing activities.

This book is not intended as a 'how-to' guide for eating garden plants. No plant or plant extract should be consumed unless you are certain of its identity and toxicity and of your potential for allergic reactions.

INTRODUCTION

I laugh now when I think of the comments my uninformed friends made years ago upon hearing of my plan to move to Alberta. Knowing my love of gardening, they asked, "Does anything grow there?" To be honest, I wasn't sure the plants I loved would grow in Alberta.

As it turned out, the more accurate question was, "What doesn't grow there?" I have found the diversity and success of gardens here in Alberta to be nothing short of astounding. Almost anything can be grown here, and many plants grow better here than they do anywhere else. Our delphiniums, for example, are stunning.

Plants have an amazing ability to adapt to varied conditions and climates. So far, almost all the plants I've tried growing in my Alberta garden have thrived, some growing even better than they did in my eastern garden. My failures have been more a result of my dog's efforts than any lack of hardiness!

The natural ecoregions of Alberta are widely diverse, ranging from open prairie grasslands to alpine meadows. Seeing what grows naturally in an area can indicate what will grow well in our gardens. This is just a starting point, however. The variety of plant material and garden designs displayed in Alberta gardens is a true indication of the bounty gardeners here have to choose from.

violas

These gardens reflect the style and enthusiasm of those determined gardeners who are willing to try anything, just to see how it will do. Many plants that are classified 'out of zone' do very well here in the right location. Every imaginable style of garden can be and has been created here, from free-form English-style cottage gardens to cool, moist, shaded woodland gardens and Zen-like Japanese gardens to formal knot gardens.

Where we garden varies almost as much as what we garden. Apartment and condo dwellers enjoy container gardening; rural gardeners may be tilling the same soil their great-grandparents did when they first came to Alberta; urban gardens include those in older neighbourhoods with deep topsoil and those whose brand new gardens may have only the thin layer of soil the construction company returned to their yards. Beautiful, successful gardens are possible in all these situations, limited only by the imagination of the gardener.

an Alberta garden

The climate is not without its challenges, and some research and experimentation are required to get the best results from your garden. Learning what to expect and when to expect it as well as what plants are best suited to your garden are key elements to gardening anywhere, not just in Alberta.

The growing season can be short, with the last and first frost dates giving us about 120 frost-free days. The long hours of daylight more than make up for the short season, providing plants with plenty of growing hours over the summer. Many plants also prefer the cool nights and low humidity that are common here.

gazanias

bridge pathway (*above*); mini alpine garden (*below*)

naturalistic water feature (*below*)

Most of Alberta is formed on an ancient seabed. Eons of flooding, draining and accumulated silt have left us with some of the best top-soil in the world. There are also some deposits of sandy soil and, in many areas, a layer of dense clay lies just beneath the topsoil. In general, the soil tends to be alkaline though some soils are acidic.

Precipitation is possibly the most variable climatic factor influencing our gardens. Though rain can be regular and adequate during the growing season, it is just as possible to experience drought conditions or excessive rain. As with all the factors that influence our gardens, we must be prepared to make the most of what nature offers us and try to take up the slack where it lets off.

Many of the garden books available to us are written by and for gardeners who have never done much cold-climate gardening. Most of the general information about gardening is accurate and useful, but hardiness information, for example, is often based on assumption and guesswork and not always on experimentation and knowledge. It is almost always worth trying a plant, even if it isn't supposed to be hardy. It may very well thrive in a sheltered spot in your garden.

The purpose of this book is to give you ideas and to help you plan out what should be done and when. Garden tasks are listed in the month they are most likely to be completed, and general ideas that can be applied in a variety of months are also included. There is plenty of space for you to write in your own thoughts and ideas.

The information in this book is general. If you need to

English wallflower with lobelia and aubretia (rockcress)

explore further to find more detailed information on a topic, you can refer to the back of the book where we have listed some resources for you. Gardening courses are offered through colleges, continuing education programs, gardening clubs and through the Master Gardener programs. You can tackle even the most daunting gardening task once you are prepared and well informed.

Use the book to keep track of unusual weather conditions, when plants sprout and when they first flower. Make a note of any unusual insects or birds you see

golden marguerite

delphinium with rudbeckia (black-eyed Susan)

in the garden. If a plant gave you a lot of trouble in a certain location, you will remember not to put it in the same location next year if you add that comment to your book. Jot down your fantastic inspirations for future garden design plans. If you see an unfamiliar and exciting plant at a garden centre or in a neighbourhood garden, you can make a note to look it up later. Write down anything about your garden that tickles your fancy. You'll appreciate it next spring when memories of last year's garden are getting a little fuzzy.

hot peppers

There are no absolute rules when it comes to gardening. No two years are identical, and all information should be taken with a pinch of salt. Use your own best judgement when deciding when to do things in your garden. If spring has been cold and wet and the soil hasn't warmed up, then wait longer before putting in plants susceptible to cold shock such as beans and tomatoes.

Above all else, always take time to enjoy your Alberta garden.

ALBERTA CLIMATE NORMALS 1971–2000
(Adapted from the Meteorological Service of Canada data
as posted on the Environment Canada website)

	CATEGORY	JAN	FEB	MAR	APR	MAY	JUN	JUL	AUG	SEP	OCT	NOV	DEC	YEAR
BANFF	DAILY MAXIMUM (°C)	-4.6	-0.4	4.5	9.5	14.5	18.5	21.9	21.3	16.3	10.1	0.2	-5.1	8.9
	DAILY MINIMUM (°C)	-14.1	-11.6	-7.3	-2.5	1.7	5.4	7.4	6.9	2.7	-1.3	-8.4	-13.3	-2.9
	RAINFALL (MM)	2.9	1.7	2.7	12.6	44.3	59.8	54.1	60.0	37.0	13.8	4.4	3.1	296.2
	SNOWFALL (CM)	34.1	29.3	28.1	22.5	17.0	1.8	0.0	0.2	5.7	19.8	32.3	43.2	234.1
	PRECIPITATION (MM)*	27.5	21.9	23.4	32.4	59.6	61.7	54.2	60.1	42.1	29.4	26.8	33.2	472.3
CALGARY	DAILY MAXIMUM (°C)	-2.8	-0.1	4.0	11.3	16.4	20.2	22.9	22.5	17.6	12.1	2.8	-1.3	10.5
	DAILY MINIMUM (°C)	-15.1	-12.0	-7.8	-2.1	3.1	7.3	9.4	8.6	4.0	-1.4	-8.9	-13.4	-2.4
	RAINFALL (MM)	0.2	0.1	1.7	11.5	51.4	79.8	67.9	58.7	41.7	6.2	1.2	0.3	320.6
	SNOWFALL (CM)	17.7	13.4	21.9	15.4	9.7	0.0	0.0	0.0	4.8	9.9	16.4	17.6	126.7
	PRECIPITATION (MM)	11.6	8.8	17.4	23.9	60.3	79.8	67.9	58.8	45.7	13.9	12.3	12.2	412.6
EDMONTON	DAILY MAXIMUM (°C)	-7.3	-3.6	2.1	11.3	17.6	21.0	22.8	22.1	16.8	10.9	0.0	-5.4	9.0
	DAILY MINIMUM (°C)	-16.0	-13.1	-7.3	-0.3	5.7	10.0	12.1	11.1	5.8	0.3	-8.2	-13.9	-1.2
	RAINFALL (MM)	1.3	0.9	2.1	13.1	45.1	87.1	91.7	68.9	42.3	10.5	1.9	0.8	365.7
	SNOWFALL (CM)	24.5	15.8	16.8	13.4	3.5	0.0	0.0	0.0	1.5	7.8	17.9	22.3	123.5
	PRECIPITATION (MM)	22.5	14.6	16.6	26.0	49.0	87.1	91.7	69.0	43.7	17.9	17.9	20.9	476.9
FT. McMURRAY	DAILY MAXIMUM (°C)	-13.6	-7.6	0.3	10.0	17.4	21.4	23.2	21.9	15.4	7.8	-4.2	-11.6	6.7
	DAILY MINIMUM (°C)	-24.0	-19.8	-13.2	-3.3	3.3	7.9	10.2	8.6	3.3	-2.2	-12.8	-21.4	-5.3
	RAINFALL (MM)	0.5	0.8	1.6	9.3	34.2	74.8	81.3	72.6	45.0	18.8	2.4	1.1	342.2
	SNOWFALL (CM)	27.0	20.6	20.4	14.5	2.9	0.0	0.0	0.0	2.4	13.1	29.0	25.9	155.8
	PRECIPITATION (MM)	19.3	15.0	16.1	21.7	36.9	74.8	81.3	72.7	46.8	29.6	22.2	19.3	455.5
GRANDE PRAIRIE	DAILY MAXIMUM (°C)	-9.5	-5.8	0.6	10.1	16.9	20.2	22.1	21.4	16.4	9.6	-1.8	-7.2	7.7
	DAILY MINIMUM (°C)	-20.5	-17.1	-10.4	-2.0	3.7	8.0	9.6	8.3	3.7	-1.7	-11.4	-17.9	-4.0
	RAINFALL (MM)	1.8	1.0	1.0	9.6	35.2	76.5	70.4	61.1	40.1	15.1	5.4	0.7	317.7
	SNOWFALL (CM)	36.4	22.5	18.6	8.7	2.0	0.0	0.0	0.7	2.8	9.4	25.5	32.0	158.6
	PRECIPITATION (MM)	30.7	18.5	15.5	17.3	36.9	76.5	70.4	61.8	42.6	23.8	26.2	26.4	446.6
HIGH LEVEL	DAILY MAXIMUM (°C)	-16.0	-10.8	-2.4	8.8	16.8	21.1	22.8	21.0	14.9	5.7	-7.7	-14.2	5.0
	DAILY MINIMUM (°C)	-27.2	-24.0	-16.8	-4.9	2.3	7.4	9.5	7.4	1.8	-4.3	-16.9	-25.2	-7.6
	RAINFALL (MM)	0.2	0.3	0.4	8.0	31.3	58.3	65.5	50.5	32.0	12.1	0.6	0.3	259.6
	SNOWFALL (CM)	24.7	20.6	20.0	8.5	5.3	0.0	0.0	0.1	2.2	18.3	30.6	25.3	155.6
	PRECIPITATION (MM)	20.3	17.7	17.3	15.6	36.4	58.3	65.5	50.6	34.4	29.7	27.4	20.9	394.1

* equivalent to rainfall

ALBERTA CLIMATE NORMALS 1971–2000
(Adapted from the Meteorological Service of Canada data
as posted on the Environment Canada website)

JASPER

CATEGORY	JAN	FEB	MAR	APR	MAY	JUN	JUL	AUG	SEP	OCT	NOV	DEC	YEAR
DAILY MAXIMUM (°C)	-5.0	-0.9	4.7	10.8	15.8	19.3	21.9	21.6	16.4	10.1	0.4	-4.8	9.2
DAILY MINIMUM (°C)	-14.6	-11.8	-7.1	-2.3	2.4	6.2	8.1	7.4	3.3	-1.2	-8.5	-13.6	-2.6
RAINFALL (MM)	4.5	2.8	5.1	12.0	28.7	54.7	60.1	59.0	35.9	22.1	8.3	3.4	296.7
SNOWFALL (CM)	30.5	18.3	16.9	8.6	1.4	0.3	0.0	0.2	1.9	8.0	21.6	30.3	138.0
PRECIPITATION (MM)	26.9	16.0	17.6	18.8	29.9	55.0	60.1	59.1	37.3	28.7	24.5	24.8	398.8

LETHBRIDGE

CATEGORY	JAN	FEB	MAR	APR	MAY	JUN	JUL	AUG	SEP	OCT	NOV	DEC	YEAR
DAILY MAXIMUM (°C)	-1.8	1.5	6.0	12.9	18.2	22.3	25.5	25.4	20.1	14.0	4.3	-0.2	12.3
DAILY MINIMUM (°C)	-13.8	-10.7	-6.5	-0.9	4.2	8.6	10.5	10.0	5.1	0.0	-7.2	-12.0	-1.1
RAINFALL (MM)	0.1	0.4	1.4	16.1	49.4	63.0	47.5	45.1	37.6	8.8	1.2	0.5	271.1
SNOWFALL (CM)	21.9	13.5	25.5	16.3	4.0	0.0	0.0	0.8	2.1	10.4	17.3	18.8	130.5
PRECIPITATION (MM)	17.6	11.6	24.0	31.3	53.5	63.0	47.5	45.8	39.6	18.9	16.9	16.7	386.3

LLOYDMINSTER

CATEGORY	JAN	FEB	MAR	APR	MAY	JUN	JUL	AUG	SEP	OCT	NOV	DEC	YEAR
DAILY MAXIMUM (°C)	-9.8	-6.8	-0.6	9.9	16.8	20.7	22.6	22.5	16.4	9.3	-3.3	-8.7	7.4
DAILY MINIMUM (°C)	-19.2	-16.4	-9.8	-1.9	3.7	8.6	10.5	9.3	3.9	-2.3	-11.5	-17.8	-3.6
RAINFALL (MM)	0.4	0.3	1.5	12.5	39.4	68.1	81.0	56.9	36.8	10.9	3.1	0.5	311.4
SNOWFALL (CM)	17.9	10.6	11.9	14.4	4.8	0.0	0.0	0.2	2.3	6.6	18.5	16.4	103.5
PRECIPITATION (MM)	16.2	10.8	12.9	26.7	43.8	68.1	81.0	57.0	39.1	17.3	19.9	15.4	408.1

MEDICINE HAT

CATEGORY	JAN	FEB	MAR	APR	MAY	JUN	JUL	AUG	SEP	OCT	NOV	DEC	YEAR
DAILY MAXIMUM (°C)	-4.5	-0.5	5.8	13.7	19.4	23.8	26.9	26.8	20.6	14.0	3.6	-2.2	12.3
DAILY MINIMUM (°C)	-15.9	-11.9	-6.4	-0.1	5.5	9.9	12.0	11.4	5.6	-0.1	-8.0	-13.6	-1.0
RAINFALL (MM)	0.5	0.3	4.5	15.6	42.7	62.6	40.6	32.9	34.6	11.7	2.7	0.9	249.6
SNOWFALL (CM)	15.9	10.7	15.0	9.6	3.2	0.0	0.0	0.4	1.5	7.0	15.2	16.6	95.2
PRECIPITATION (MM)	13.7	9.3	18.3	24.8	46.0	62.6	40.6	33.3	36.2	18.5	15.8	14.7	333.8

PEACE RIVER

CATEGORY	JAN	FEB	MAR	APR	MAY	JUN	JUL	AUG	SEP	OCT	NOV	DEC	YEAR
DAILY MAXIMUM (°C)	-11.4	-7.1	0.0	9.9	17.0	20.4	22.2	21.2	15.7	8.4	-3.4	-9.0	7.0
DAILY MINIMUM (°C)	-21.9	-18.3	-11.8	-2.6	3.4	7.9	9.7	8.1	3.3	-2.4	-12.5	-19.3	-4.7
RAINFALL (MM)	0.4	0.4	0.8	9.7	32.8	70.9	66.6	55.3	38.5	14.8	3.5	0.6	294.2
SNOWFALL (CM)	23.1	18.2	14.0	6.7	2.5	0.0	0.0	0.2	2.5	9.9	19.8	22.5	119.3
PRECIPITATION (MM)	21.3	16.4	13.3	16.1	35.4	70.9	66.6	55.4	40.5	24.3	21.3	20.7	402.3

RED DEER

CATEGORY	JAN	FEB	MAR	APR	MAY	JUN	JUL	AUG	SEP	OCT	NOV	DEC	YEAR
DAILY MAXIMUM (°C)	-5.8	-2.7	2.9	11.3	16.9	20.5	22.6	21.9	17.5	11.7	1.4	-4.1	9.5
DAILY MINIMUM (°C)	-17.4	-14.8	-8.8	-1.8	3.8	8.0	10.1	8.8	4.1	-1.3	-9.4	-15.0	-2.8
RAINFALL (MM)	0.6	0.2	0.8	14.3	59.4	84.1	92.2	70.1	47.1	14.4	1.9	0.3	385.3
SNOWFALL (CM)	21.7	11.0	18.7	7.2	2.4	0.0	0.0	0.0	1.9	5.7	15.7	17.4	101.8
PRECIPITATION (MM)	22.4	11.2	19.6	21.5	61.8	84.1	92.2	70.1	49.0	20.1	17.5	17.8	487.2

ALBERTA CLIMATE EXTREMES 1971–2000
(Adapted from the Meteorological Service of Canada data
as posted on the Environment Canada website)

BANFF

MAXIMUM (°C)	34.4 ON JULY 28, 1934
MINIMUM (°C)	-51.2 ON JANUARY 25, 1950
DAILY RAINFALL (MM)	53.1 ON JULY 13, 1948
DAILY SNOWFALL (CM)	58.6 ON DECEMBER 14, 1979
SNOW DEPTH (CM)	132.0 ON MARCH 1, 1972

JASPER

MAXIMUM (°C)	36.7 ON JULY 16, 1941
MINIMUM (°C)	-46.7 ON JANUARY 19, 1935
DAILY RAINFALL (MM)	107.7 ON AUGUST 5, 1969
DAILY SNOWFALL (CM)	51.6 ON FEBRUARY 17, 1948
SNOW DEPTH (CM)	94.0 ON FEBRUARY 1, 1974

CALGARY

MAXIMUM (°C)	36.1 ON JULY 15, 1919
MINIMUM (°C)	-45.0 ON FEBRUARY 4, 1893
DAILY RAINFALL (MM)	95.3 ON JULY 15, 1927
DAILY SNOWFALL (CM)	48.4 ON MAY 6, 1981
SNOW DEPTH (CM)	38.0 ON MARCH 18, 1998

LETHBRIDGE

MAXIMUM (°C)	39.4 ON JULY 10, 1973
MINIMUM (°C)	-42.8 ON JANUARY 3, 1950
DAILY RAINFALL (MM)	85.4 ON MAY 23, 1980
DAILY SNOWFALL (CM)	55.1 ON SEPTEMBER 21, 1968
SNOW DEPTH (CM)	86.0 ON APRIL 30, 1967

EDMONTON

MAXIMUM (°C)	34.5 ON AUGUST 5, 1998
MINIMUM (°C)	-48.3 ON DECEMBER 28, 1938
DAILY RAINFALL (MM)	114.0 ON JULY 31, 1953
DAILY SNOWFALL (CM)	39.9 ON NOVEMBER 15, 1942
SNOW DEPTH (CM)	84.0 ON MARCH 18, 1974

LLOYDMINSTER

MAXIMUM (°C)	37.4 ON AUGUST 5, 1998
MINIMUM (°C)	-42.5 ON FEBRUARY 7, 1994
DAILY RAINFALL (MM)	63.4 ON JULY 29, 1986
DAILY SNOWFALL (CM)	57.6 ON APRIL 27, 1991
SNOW DEPTH (CM)	49.0 ON JANUARY 29, 1997

FT. McMURRAY

MAXIMUM (°C)	37.0 ON AUGUST 10, 1991
MINIMUM (°C)	-50.6 ON FEBRUARY 1, 1947
DAILY RAINFALL (MM)	94.5 ON AUGUST 6, 1976
DAILY SNOWFALL (CM)	29.7 ON MARCH 16, 1951
SNOW DEPTH (CM)	68.0 ON JANUARY 13, 1996

MEDICINE HAT

MAXIMUM (°C)	42.2 ON JULY 12, 1886
MINIMUM (°C)	-46.1 ON JANUARY 22, 1886
DAILY RAINFALL (MM)	121.9 ON AUGUST 14, 1927
DAILY SNOWFALL (CM)	33.8 ON MARCH 11, 1954
SNOW DEPTH (CM)	50.0 ON NOVEMBER 26, 1990

GRANDE PRAIRIE

MAXIMUM (°C)	34.5 ON AUGUST 9, 1981
MINIMUM (°C)	-52.2 ON JANUARY 2, 1950
DAILY RAINFALL (MM)	90.0 ON AUGUST 5, 1994
DAILY SNOWFALL (CM)	36.3 ON OCTOBER 4, 1957
SNOW DEPTH (CM)	86.0 ON FEBRUARY 1, 1982

PEACE RIVER

MAXIMUM (°C)	36.7 ON JULY 13, 1945
MINIMUM (°C)	-49.4 ON JANUARY 13, 1950
DAILY RAINFALL (MM)	53.0 ON MAY 4, 2000
DAILY SNOWFALL (CM)	26.2 ON APRIL 12, 1966
SNOW DEPTH (CM)	117.0 ON APRIL 1, 1967

HIGH LEVEL

MAXIMUM (°C)	35.2 ON AUGUST 9, 1981
MINIMUM (°C)	-50.6 ON JANUARY 13, 1972
DAILY RAINFALL (MM)	103.4 ON JULY 13, 1998
DAILY SNOWFALL (CM)	42.6 ON MAY 20, 1989
SNOW DEPTH (CM)	104.0 ON MARCH 19, 1987

RED DEER

MAXIMUM (°C)	36.0 ON AUGUST 5, 1998
MINIMUM (°C)	-43.3 ON DECEMBER 9, 1977
DAILY RAINFALL (MM)	97.4 ON JULY 29, 1981
DAILY SNOWFALL (CM)	28.5 ON SEPTEMBER 17, 1997
SNOW DEPTH (CM)	75.0 ON MARCH 3, 1997

ALBERTA
LAST SPRING FROST DATES
■ BEFORE MAY 21
■ MAY 21 – MAY 31
■ MAY 31 – JUNE 11
■ JUNE 11 – JUNE 21
■ JUNE 21 – JULY 1
■ AFTER JULY 1

ALBERTA
FIRST FALL FROST DATES
■ BEFORE SEPTEMBER 1
■ SEPTEMBER 1 – SEPTEMBER 11
■ SEPTEMBER 11 – SEPTEMBER 21
■ AFTER SEPTEMBER 21

JANUARY

*Now is the time for planning and
dreaming of the distant summer
and the garden yet to be.*

JANUARY

1

2

Avoid using chemical de-icers because they are harmful to lawns and garden plants.

3

4

If you had a real Christmas tree, an alternative to recycling is to cut it up and use the branches as a mulch to shelter low-growing shrubs and groundcovers.

5

6

7

One of the flowers you might dream of adding to your garden in spring is the beautiful hybrid 'Loving Memory' (*left*). Though a zone 5 rose, it can flourish in an Alberta garden in a sheltered spot and with a little extra care.

Mountain ash (*right*)

In a good year, the garden is blanketed in snow by January, but just as likely the ground may still lie bare, exposed to the extremes of our northern climate. South-facing walls are always warmer than other areas of the garden. Snow melts most quickly here, leaving plants vulnerable to the stressful cycles of heat and cold. A good, thick fall mulch proves to be worth its weight in gold in a snowless year or a snowless area.

THINGS TO DO

January is one of the hardest months for the garden and the easiest for the gardener.

Water shrubs and evergreens during winter thaws if there is no snow around them. Water the ground around the plants, but don't worry if some water freezes onto the branches—the ice won't hurt them.

Don't forget to top up your bird-feeders regularly. Feeding the birds encourages them to keep visiting in summer when they will help keep your insect pest populations under control.

Snow is the garden's best friend. Pile clean snow on snowless garden beds to insulate them against the wind and cold. Some people refer to this as "snow farming."

JANUARY

8

9

Avoid placing houseplants in hot or cold drafts.

10

11

Order gardening and seed catalogues to look through even if you don't start your own seeds.

12

13

14

Begonias (*left*) can be brought indoors in fall and kept as houseplants in a sunny location through the winter.

Gently brush snow off the branches of evergreens such as cedars, but leave any ice that forms to melt naturally. The weight of the snow or ice can permanently bend flexible branches, but more damage is done trying to remove ice than is done through its weight.

Choose and order seeds for early starting. Sort through the seeds you have, test them for viability and throw out any that don't germinate or that you won't grow. Trade seeds with gardening friends.

Get lawn mowers and other power tools serviced now. They will be ready for use in spring, and you may get a better price before the spring rush.

Annual poppy seeds are easy to collect and share with friends. There are many colour choices available in both single- (*Iceland poppies, centre right*) and double-flowering (*peony-flowered poppies, top right and bottom*) varieties.

To test older seeds for viability, place 10 seeds between two layers of moist paper towel and put them in a sealed container. Keep the paper evenly dampened but not too wet. Seeds may rot if the paper towel is too moist. Check each day to see if the seeds have sprouted. If less than half the seeds sprout, buy new ones.

15

16

*Reduce watering of houseplants because
most need little water during winter.*

17

18

19

20

The datura (*left*) is an elegant, exotic-looking plant
that produces large, showy, scented flowers. Daturas
are relatively new to the Alberta garden scene.

Clean the foliage of your house-plants. When light levels are low, it is important for plants to be able to use whatever light is available. As a bonus, you might help reduce insect populations because their eggs will be wiped off along with the dust.

Check houseplants regularly for common indoor insect pests such as whiteflies, spider mites and mealybugs.

GARDEN DESIGN

As you look out your windows at the frozen yard, think about what could make your garden look attractive in winter. Persistent fruit, unusual bark and branch patterns, evergreens and colourfully stemmed shrubs provide winter interest.

Coleus (*top right*)
English ivy topiary (*bottom right*)

Most indoor plants will benefit from increased humidity levels. Place pots on a tray of pebbles. If you add water to the pebbles when needed, you will increase the humidity through evaporation but prevent water-logged roots.

JANUARY

21

22

January is a great time for garden planning. In winter, the bones of the garden are laid bare, so you can take a good look at the garden's overall structure.

23

24

25

26

27

Rosehips (*left*); the coppery bark of amur cherry and the bright berries of viburnum (*top right*); the seedpods of amur maple (*centre right*); and the peeling bark of birch (*bottom right*) add interest to the garden in winter.

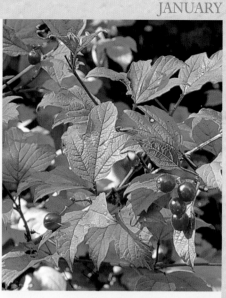

Plants that add variety to a winter garden

- Shrub Roses (*Rosa*): brightly coloured hips
- Dogwoods (*Cornus*): red, purple or yellow stems
- Amur Maple (*Acer ginnala*): attractive bark; branching pattern
- Winged Euonymus (*Euonymus alatus*): corky ridges on the branches
- Highbush Cranberry (*Viburnum trilobum*): bright red berries
- Cedar (*Thuja*) or Juniper (*Juniperus*): evergreen branches
- Weeping Birch (*Betula pendula*): pendulous branches; attractive white bark; contrasting young red branches
- Clematis (*Clematis*): fuzzy seedheads
- Mountain Ash (*Sorbus*): persistent red berries
- Amur Cherry (*Prunus maackii*): coppery, peeling bark

JANUARY

*Imagine the garden you'd like to have,
and keep a notebook and your diagrams
at hand so you can jot down ideas
as they come to you.*

Woody evergreens, such as cedar (*below*), upright juniper (*top right*) and white spruce (*far right*), add interesting texture and rich green colour to a sometimes monotonous winter landscape.

PROBLEM AREAS IN THE GARDEN

Keep track of these potential problem areas in your garden.

- windswept areas: perhaps a tree, shrub or hedge could be added next summer to provide shelter

- snowfree areas: places where the snow is always quick to melt are poor choices for very tender plants, which benefit most from the protection of the snow

- snowbound areas: places where the snow is slowest to melt provide the most protection to plants but stay frozen longest in spring, making them poor locations for spring-flowering plants

Spruce are widely grown in Alberta, and newer varieties are available almost every gardening season. They are well suited to our winters, and some, such as the Colorado blue spruce *(left)*, provide rich green colour against brilliant white snow.

FEBRUARY

The longer days and occasional warm spells turn our thoughts to the upcoming gardening season.

FEBRUARY

1

2

*Finish ordering plants and seeds
from catalogues.*

3

4

*During warm spells, water plants
not covered by snow.*

5

6

7

Colourful little crabapples often remain on the
branches of the tree through winter, a reminder of
the beautiful blossoms to come in spring
(*left and top right*).
Flowering crabapple trees in spring
(*bottom right*)

Groundhog Day is a celebration we have trouble relating to because shadow or no shadow, we've always got six more weeks of winter at the beginning of February. Gardening can get under way, however. February is a great month for starting seeds and keeping a close eye on the garden during those warm, potentially dry spells.

THINGS TO DO

February is another month with few tasks, but preparations can be made now that will keep things moving smoothly once the season kicks into high gear.

Check shrubs and trees for storm-damaged branches, and remove them using proper pruning techniques.

Cut branches of flowering shrubs, such as forsythia, crabapple and cherry, to bring indoors. Placed in a bright location in a vase of water, they will begin to flower, giving you a taste of spring in winter.

FEBRUARY

8

9

Continue to check for insect pests on your houseplants.

10

11

Thoroughly clean empty planters, containers and seed trays to get them ready for spring planting.

12

13

14

Hollyhock (*left*), browallia (*top right*), bellflower (*far right*) and begonia (*near right*) are plants you can start from seed in February.

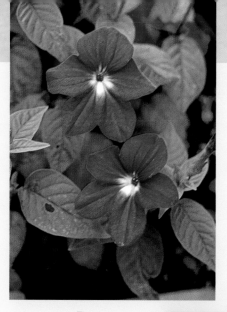

Start seeds for annuals, perennials and vegetables that are slow to mature. A few to consider are

- Geranium (*Pelargonium*)
- Amethyst Flower (*Browallia*)
- Bellflower (*Campanula*)
- Begonia (*Begonia*)
- Hollyhock (*Alcea*)
- Lady's Mantle (*Alchemilla*)
- Pinks (*Dianthus*)
- Tomatoes (*Lycopersicon*)
- Peppers (*Capsicum*)

Starting plants from seed is a great way to propagate a large number of plants at a relatively low cost. You can grow plants you can't find at any garden centre and get a jump-start on the growing season.

FEBRUARY

15

16

Keep seedlings in the brightest location available to reduce stretching.

17

18

Check to see if any of the tubers or bulbs you are storing indoors have started sprouting. Pot them and keep them in a bright location once they do.

19

20

Many varieties of dahlia (*below*) can be started from seed in February for transplanting after the danger of frost has passed.

Carnations (*centre right*) can be seeded indoors; seed tray, pots, soil and spray mister for indoor seeding (*bottom right*)

21

As the days start to lengthen, indoor plants may start to show signs of new growth. Increase watering and apply a weak fertilizer (1/4 strength) only after they begin to grow.

Seedlings will be weak and floppy if they don't get enough light. Consider purchasing a fluorescent or other grow light (*above*) to provide extra illumination for them.

STARTING SEEDS

There are a few things you will need for starting seeds:

- containers to grow them in, such as pots, trays or peat pots
- sterile soil mix intended for starting seeds
- plastic bags or tray covers to keep the seedbed humid.

Tips for growing healthy seedlings:

- Transplant seedlings to individual containers once they have three or four true leaves to prevent crowding.
- Space plants so that the leaves do not overshadow those of neighbouring plants.

22

23

After seeds have been planted, and once seedlings emerge, moisten the soil with a hand-held spray mister when the soil begins to dry out.

24

25

Don't fertilize young seedlings. Wait until the seed leaves (the first leaves to appear) have begun to shrivel, then fertilize with a weak fertilizer once a week.

26

27

28

29

The floribunda rose 'Fellowship/Livin' Easy' (*left*) is well known for its reliable vigour, attractive foliage and showy, long-lived blooms. It also makes a great cut flower.

Tips for starting seeds:

- Moisten the soil before you fill the containers.
- Firm the soil down in the containers, but don't pack it too tightly.
- Leave seeds that require light for germination uncovered.
- Plant large seeds individually by poking a hole in the soil with the tip of a pen or pencil and then dropping the seed in the hole.
- Spread small seeds evenly across the soil surface, then lightly cover with more soil mix.
- To spread small seeds, place them in the crease of a folded piece of paper and gently tap the bottom of the fold to roll them onto the soil (*top right*).
- Mix very tiny seeds, like those of begonia, with very fine sand before planting to spread them out more evenly.
- Plant only one type of seed in each container. Some seeds will germinate before others, and it is difficult to keep both seeds and seedlings happy in the same container.
- Cover pots or trays of seeds with clear plastic to keep them moist (*bottom right*).
- Seeds do not need bright, direct light to germinate and can be kept in an out-of-the-way place until they begin to sprout.
- Once the seeds germinate, keep the seedlings in a bright location and remove the plastic cover.

A hand-held spray mister and a heating coil or pad are useful, but not required.

To prevent seedlings from damping-off, always use a sterile soil mix, thoroughly clean containers before using them, maintain good air circulation around seedlings and water from the bottom, keeping the soil moist, not soggy.

FEBRUARY

Envision the garden you want rather than the garden you have by designing your own garden layout (*below*). Garden design can be as simple as planting a container to display on your patio or deck, or it can be more complex, involving a variety of beds and borders or the addition of features such as shelters and walkways (*opposite page*).

N

FLOWERBED

FLOWERING CRABAPPLE

PATIO

HOUSE

FLOWERBED

WALKWAY

FLOWERBED

WEEPING BIRCH

DRIVEWAY

GARDEN PLANNING

Using graph paper, plot out the existing yard and house:

- Put in trees, shrubs and other solid structural elements. If you remember where the flowerbeds are, add those as well. Garden beds can be added later if you're not sure. Make copies and use them to keep track of your plans.

- Create a master plan and then sub-plans so you can keep track of the changes you'd like to make each year.

- Make another plan of just your vegetable garden, if you have one, so you can plan and keep track of crop rotations.

MARCH

Expect the unexpected in March. Our gardens can be under a blanket of snow one year or showing the first signs of spring in another.

MARCH

1

2

Prune off any growth on your trees and shrubs that was damaged over winter.

3

4

The single most important thing you can do when planting is to make sure you have the right plant in the right location. Consider the mature size of the plant and its cultural requirements.

5

6

When designing your garden, consider planting a fast-growing, drought-tolerant elder (*left and near right*). The elder's showy foliage adds colour and texture to a landscape, and its edible berries can be made into jelly or wine or left for the birds.

Prune red-twig dogwoods (*top right and far right*) in spring.

7

Though we may experience some very spring-like weather in March, it is usually in our garden's best interest to keep the plants dormant for just a little longer. Frost and snow can quickly kill unsuspecting early starters when the weather takes a turn for the worse.

THINGS TO DO

The first few tasks of spring get us out in the garden by late March.

Days can be warm enough to encourage some plants to start sprouting. Keep snow piled on beds or mulches topped up to protect plants from the freezing nights.

MARCH

8

9

As the snow begins to melt, start clearing up the debris in your yard, such as leaves, sticks, garbage and doggie poop.

10

11

Prune late-flowering shrubs (July or later) and shrubs grown for colourful young growth.

12

13

As soon as the snow begins to melt in spring, the leaves of the bergenia become visible and are quickly followed by its pretty magenta flowers (*left*).

Spirea (*top right*); hardy kiwi (*centre right*); hydrangea (*bottom right*)

14

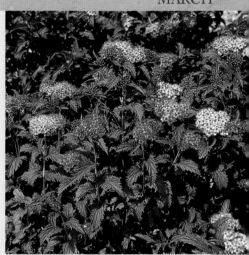

Keep off your lawn when it is frozen, bare of snow and/or very wet to avoid damaging the grass or compacting the soil.

Apply horticultural oil (also called dormant oil), used to control over-wintering insects, to trees, shrubs and vines before the buds swell. Follow the directions carefully to avoid harming beneficial insects.

Plants to prune in spring
- Red-twig Dogwood (*Cornus alba*)
- Yellow or Purple-leafed Elders (*Sambucus*)
- Hydrangea (*Hydrangea*)
- Hardy Kiwi (*Actinidia arguta*)
- Potentilla (*Potentilla*)
- Japanese Spirea (*Spirea japonica*)
- False Spirea (*Sorbaria sorbifolia*)

MARCH

15

16

Start indoor seeding. Most of the seeds you may wish to start early can be started by late March.

17

18

Water houseplants that start sprouting new growth more frequently, and apply a weak fertilizer.

19

20

21

Peegee hydrangea (*left*) is a popular and adaptable shrub that grows well in a protected site with moist soil. It is lovely in full bloom.

If planted early enough in spring, clematis (*top right*) flowers the first summer.

PLANTING IN SPRING

As March draws to a close, we head into prime planting season. Trees, shrubs, vines and perennials often establish most quickly when they are planted just as they are about to break dormancy. They are full of growth hormones, and they recover quickly from transplant shock.

Avoid using dormant oil on blue-needled evergreens, such as blue spruce (*above and below*). The treatment takes the blue off the existing needles, though the new needles will be blue.

22

23

Before doing any digging, call your utility companies to locate any buried wires, cables or pipes to prevent injury and save time and money.

24

25

Don't plant vigorous spreaders in rock gardens with tiny alpine plants or large shrubs right next to walkways.

26

27

28

Blue Himalayan poppies (*left*) grow well in the right conditions in Alberta but are rarer in the rest of Canada. They prefer partial shade and rich, moist soil and look good near a water feature.

Welsh poppies near water feature (*top right*); hazel (*bottom right*)

A few things to keep in mind when planting your garden:

- Never work with your soil when it is very wet or very dry.

- Avoid planting during the hottest, sunniest part of the day. Choose an overcast day, or plant early or late in the day.

- Prepare your soil before you plant to avoid damaging roots later.

- Get your new plants into the ground as soon as possible when you get them home. Roots can get hot and dry out quickly in containers. Keep plants in a shady spot if you must wait to plant them.

- Most plants are happiest when planted at the same depth they have always grown at. Trees, in particular, can be killed by too deep a planting.

- Remove containers before planting. Plastic and fibre pots restrict root growth and prevent plants from becoming established.

- Plants should be well watered when they are newly planted. Watering deeply and infrequently will encourage the strongest root growth.

- Check the root zone before watering. The soil surface may appear dry when the roots are still moist.

MARCH

29

30

31

If a plant needs well-drained soil and full sun to thrive, it will be healthiest and best able to fight off problems in those conditions. Work with your plants' natural tendencies.

The splendid yellow shrub rose 'Morden Sunrise' (*below*) is one of the few yellow roses hardy enough for Alberta gardens.

Harden annuals and perennials off before planting them by gradually exposing them to longer periods of time outside. Doing so gives your plants time to adapt to outdoor weather conditions and reduces the chance of transplant shock.

Remove only damaged branches when planting trees or shrubs, and leave the plant to settle in for at least one year before you begin any formative pruning. Plants need all the branches and leaves they have when they are trying to get established.

Trees less than 1.5 m (5') tall do not need staking unless they are in a very windy location. Unstaked trees develop stronger root systems.

staking a tree properly

planting a balled-and-burlapped tree

planting a bare-root tree

APRIL

Though April can be unpredictable,
we can't help feeling that spring is
finally here.

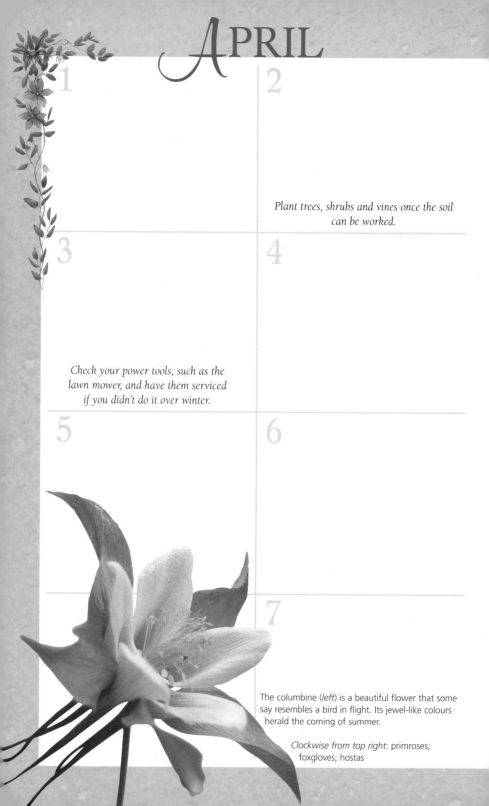

APRIL

1

2

Plant trees, shrubs and vines once the soil can be worked.

3

4

Check your power tools, such as the lawn mower, and have them serviced if you didn't do it over winter.

5

6

7

The columbine (*left*) is a beautiful flower that some say resembles a bird in flight. Its jewel-like colours herald the coming of summer.

Clockwise from top right: primroses; foxgloves; hostas

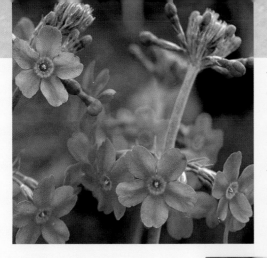

Take a trip to a garden centre. The best selection of uncommon annuals and perennials is available early, and you may be able to purchase woody plants while they are still dormant. Many garden centres will take your name and call you when the plants you are looking for arrive.

The first warm days of spring are a welcome sign, but we know that cold, frosty nights and perhaps a late spring snowfall are just as likely. The first green shoots start to emerge, and we become eager to get out in the garden.

April frosts are almost inevitable, but by the end of the month we feel assured that warm days and summer are just around the corner. We finish our tidying and watch as our gardens begin to awaken.

APRIL

8

9

Pull back mulch from sprouting plants on warm days, but be prepared to cover plants back over on cold nights.

10

11

Clean up the garden once the snow has melted. Rake debris off lawns and prune back old perennial growth.

12

13

14

Consider planting daylilies (*left*) this spring. Though the blooms last only a day, these lilies are easygoing, prolific and versatile and come in an almost infinite variety of forms, sizes and colours.

Godetia (*top right*) and California poppies (*bottom right*) can be sown directly into the garden in spring.

THINGS TO DO

The real gardening work begins—raking, digging, planting and pruning. We begin the hard work that will let us sit back and enjoy the garden once summer arrives.

Bring garden tools out of storage and examine them for rust or other damage. Clean and sharpen them if you didn't before you put them away in fall.

Store any plants you have purchased or started indoors in as bright a location as possible. You may begin to harden them off by placing them outdoors for a short period each day.

Avoid working your soil until it has thawed and dried out a bit. A handful of thawed soil should squeeze into a ball that holds its shape but breaks easily apart when pressed with a thumb or finger.

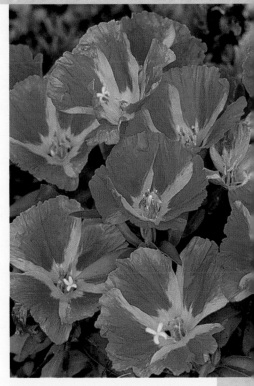

Seeds sown directly into the garden may take longer to germinate than those planted indoors, but the resulting plants will be stronger.

APRIL

15

16

Divide perennials that bloom in mid-summer or later, such as asters, daylilies and sedums.

17

18

April can be windy and, once the snow melts, very dry. It is vital to keep plants well watered when they are breaking dormancy to prevent the new shoots from drying out.

19

20

21

A traditional garden favourite, sweet peas (*left*) are easy to grow from seed in spring. They sprout quickly and have sweetly scented blooms that can be cut often for fragrant indoor bouquets.

Clockwise from top right: phlox, cabbage, rocket larkspur and nigella be planted before the last spring frost.

Warming up vegetable beds with row covers allows many plants and seeds to be sown early.

Many plants prefer to grow in cool weather and can be started well before the last frost. These seeds can be planted as soon as the soil can be worked:

- Spinach (*Spinacea oleracea*)
- Peas (*Pisum sativum*)
- Swiss Chard (*Beta vulgaris*)
- Cabbage (*Brassica oleracea*)
- Kale (*Brassica napus*)
- Bachelor's Buttons (*Centaurea cyanus*)
- Calendula (*Calendula officinalis*)
- California Poppy (*Eschscholzia californica*)
- Godetia (*Clarkia amoena*)
- Love-in-a-Mist (*Nigella damascena*)
- Phlox (*Phlox drummondii*)
- Poppy (*Papaver rhoeas*)
- Rocket Larkspur (*Consolida ajacis*)
- Sweet Pea (*Lathyrus odoratus*)

APRIL

22

23

Repot houseplants if needed.

24

25

Tomatoes, snapdragons and spiderflowers can be started from seed only a few weeks before moving them into the garden.

26

27

28

You can depend on aubretia (*left*) to put on a great floral show in spring.

Clockwise from top right: spiral juniper; pom-pom juniper; an example of formal pruning

PRUNING

Prune trees and shrubs to maintain the health and attractive shape of a plant, increase the quality and yield of fruit, control and direct growth and create interesting plant forms and shapes.

Once you learn how to prune plants correctly, it is an enjoyable garden task. There are many good books available on the topic of pruning. One is listed at the back of this book. If you are unsure about pruning, take a pruning course, often offered by garden centres, botanical gardens and adult education courses.

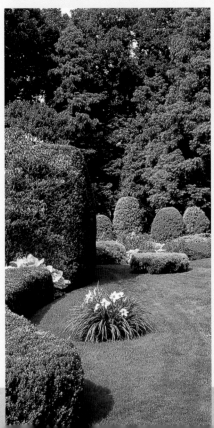

Don't prune trees or shrubs when growth has started and buds are swelling. Prune before growth starts in spring or wait until plants have leafed out.

Clockwise from top right: climbing rose with support; espalier; proper secateur orientation

PRUNING TIPS

■ Prune at the right time of year. Trees and shrubs that flower before June, usually on the previous year's wood, should be pruned after they have flowered. Trees and shrubs that flower after June, usually on new growth, can be pruned in spring.

■ Use the correct tool for the size of branch to be removed: secateurs, or hand pruners, for growth up to 2 cm (3/4") in diameter; long-handled loppers for growth up to 4 cm (1½") in diameter; or a pruning saw for growth up to about 15 cm (6") in diameter.

■ Always use clean and sharp tools.

■ Always use secateurs or loppers with the blade side towards the plant and the hook towards the part to be removed.

thinning cuts

Thin trees and shrubs to promote the growth of younger, healthier branches. Doing so rejuvenates a plant.

correct

too low

angle too great

too high

When pruning, avoid the following:

- Don't leave stubs. Whether you are cutting off a large branch or deadheading a lilac, always cut back to a join. Branches should be removed to the branch collar, and smaller growth should be cut back to a bud or branch union. There is no absolute set angle for pruning. Each plant should be pruned according to its individual needs.

- Never use pruning paint or paste. Trees have a natural ability to create a barrier between living and dead wood. Painting over a cut impairs this ability.

- Never try to remove a tree or large branch by yourself. Have someone help you, or hire a professional to do it.

Always hire an ISA (International Society of Arboriculture) certified professional to remove branches on trees growing near power lines or other hazardous areas, especially if they could damage a building, fence or car if they were to fall. Branches and trees are usually much heavier than anticipated and can do a lot of damage if they fall in the wrong place.

MAY

*The promise of spring is fulfilled with
the sprouting and blooming of May,
and winter is soon forgotten.*

MAY

1

2

Move or divide any perennials that didn't have enough space last summer.

3

4

Prune early-flowering shrubs, such as forsythia, once they are finished flowering, if needed.

5

6

7

The Japanese anemone or windflower (*left*) is a delight in spring and fall, when it puts on a charming floral display.

Stake or put hoops around peonies (*far right*) now so these will be hidden as the foliage fills in. The combination of tulips and pansies (*bottom right*) makes an interesting colour and height contrast in a spring flowerbed.

May weather can still be unpredictable, one year warm and sunny and the next frosty and threatening flurries. In a typical May, bulbs are blooming, peonies poke up their red and green spears, and forsythias burst forth in a riot of yellow. Even the most devoted lawn-lover knows that spring is truly here when the first dandelion, tucked up against a south wall, opens its fuzzy face to the sun.

THINGS TO DO

A new gardening season awaits, one where we haven't forgotten to weed or water, where all our plants are properly spaced and well staked and where no insects have chewed any leaves. Now is the time to finish tidying up the garden, prepare the garden beds and get the planting done.

MAY

8

Begin to harden off any houseplants you plan to move outdoors for summer.

9

10

11

Work compost into your garden beds and fork them over, removing weeds as you go, to prepare them for planting later in the month.

12

13

14

Clematis such as C. 'Gravetye Beauty' (*left*) is a popular perennial vine with beautiful, showy flowers in many shapes and sizes. By planting a variety of them, you can have clematis in bloom from spring to fall.

Clockwise from top right: C. 'Hagley hybrid'; C. *integrifolia*; C. 'Etoile Violette'

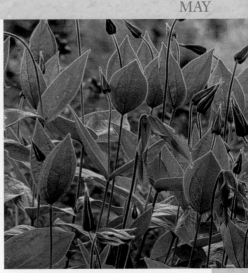

Remove mulch from perennials and trim back and clear away any of last year's growth if it was still too cold to do so in April.

Clear away any of the annuals or vegetables that didn't make it to the compost pile last fall.

By the end of the month, you will have a good idea of what has been damaged or killed back over winter, and you can trim or remove plants as needed.

Accept that grass will not grow everywhere. Grass requires plenty of sun and regular moisture. Many trees and buildings provide too much shade and don't allow enough water to penetrate the soil for grass to grow successfully. Use mulch or other groundcovers in areas where you have trouble growing grass. When selecting trees to plant in the lawn, choose ones that will provide only light shade and that will enjoy the plentiful water they will be sharing with the grass, or have a grass-free zone extending from the base of the tree to the dripline.

15

16

Continue to harden off your early-started seedlings and purchased plants so they will be ready to plant outside when the weather is warm enough.

17

18

When planning your vegetable garden, consider planting extra to donate to a local food bank or homeless shelter. Even if you just end up with the inevitable extra zucchini and tomatoes, they can be put to good use.

19

20

21

Plant a sunny spring flower such as doronicum (*left*) with tulips and forget-me-nots to create a cheerful May display.

It is possible to have a healthy, attractive organic lawn. Grass is an extremely competitive plant, capable of fighting off invasions by weeds, pests and diseases without the use of chemicals.

Lawns need very little water to remain green. Watering deeply and infrequently will encourage deep roots that are not easily damaged during periods of drought. Five millimetres (1/4") of water a week will keep grass alive and 2.5 cm (1") a week will keep it green (*below*).

The official last frost date for most Alberta gardens is May 24, but don't limit yourself to planting only on or after this date. Judge the planting by how the year is progressing. In a warm year, when nights stay above freezing, even early in the month, it is worth putting in a few of the more tender plants, such as tomatoes. If there are no more frosts, you will have gained several weeks on our short growing season. In a cool year you may even wait until after May 24 before planting tender heat-lovers, such as beans (*left*), to give the soil more time to warm.

22

23

Start new garden beds or expand and improve old ones.

24

25

De-thatch lawns in spring only when the thatch layer is more than 2 cm (3/4") deep.

26

27

28

Despite their exotic appearance, hostas (*left*) flourish in Alberta gardens. A wide variety will grow and thrive here in light shade and rich, moist soil.

TURFGRASS

Turfgrass aficionados are having a hard time these days. Cities across Canada are taking steps to ban pesticide use on lawns, and summer water bans leave turf dry and crisp during hot spells. Alternative groundcovers and xeriscapes are being hailed as the way of the future, but there are positives to turfgrasses that make them worth keeping. Lawns efficiently filter pollutants out of run-off water, prevent soil erosion, retain moisture, cool the air and resist drought.

Although lawns require a layer of thatch to improve wear tolerance, reduce compaction and insulate against weather extremes, too thick a thatch layer can prevent water absorption, make the grass susceptible to heat, drought and cold and encourage pest and disease problems.

May-blooming flowers: (*clockwise from top*) irises bloom in early spring; forget-me-nots bloom once in spring, and flowers reappear all summer long; rockcress flowers attract bees and butterflies in spring and look exceptional in rock gardens.

31

May is the perfect time to plant such vegetables as beans, beets, leaf lettuce, peas, potatoes, radishes and spinach. They are easy to grow from seed and mature quickly.

Forget-me-nots (*left*), rockcress (*top right*) and bergenia (*bottom right*) are easy-to-grow, reliable bloomers and perfect for beginner gardeners.

Here are some tips for maintaining a healthy, organic lawn:

- Aerate your lawn in spring, after active growth begins, to relieve compaction and allow water and air to move freely through the soil.

- Feed the soil, not the plants. Organic fertilizers or compost will encourage a healthy population of soil microbes. These work with roots to provide plants with nutrients and to fight off attacks by pests and diseases. Apply an organic fertilizer in late spring after you aerate the lawn and in fall just as the grass goes dormant.

- Mow lawns to a height of 5 to 6 cm (2–2½"). If kept this height, the remaining blade will shade the ground, preventing moisture loss,

keeping roots cooler, reducing the stress the grass suffers from being mowed and helping the grass out-compete weeds for space and sunlight.

- Grass clippings should be left on the lawn to return their nutrients to the soil and add organic matter. Mowing your lawn once a week or as often as needed during the vigorous growing season will ensure that the clippings decompose quickly.

- Healthy turfgrass will out-compete most weeds. Remove weeds by hand. If you must use chemicals, apply them only to the weeds. Chemical herbicides disrupt the balance of soil microbes and are not necessary to have a healthy lawn.

JUNE

The long, warm days
of summer are with us, and the
garden flourishes.

JUNE

1

2

Plant tender transplants such as pumpkins, tomatoes, begonias and coleus.

3

4

Heat-loving plants such as beans and marigolds will germinate quickly in the warm soil. Direct sow early in June.

5

6

7

Cranesbill geraniums (*left*) are charming late spring flowers with attractive foliage. The leaves of some varieties emit a lemon-mint scent.

Petunias with English ivy (*top right*) in an urn-shaped planter; daylilies (*bottom right*) planted en masse serve as a screen.

In June, the grass is green, flower-beds are filling and perennials, trees and shrubs are blooming. We watch as seeds germinate and leaves unfold. The fear of frost is behind us, and the soil is warm enough for even the most tender plants. Rain is usually plentiful in June, but in a dry year, newly planted annuals and perennials may need supplemental watering until they become established.

THINGS TO DO

June is the month to finish up the planting and begin the general maintenance work that will keep larger projects to a minimum.

Stake plants before they fill in if you haven't already done so.

Apply mulch to shrub, perennial and vegetable beds. Doing so will shade the roots and reduce the amount of water the plants will require.

Pinch late-flowering perennials back lightly to encourage bushier growth and more flowers.

If you haven't done so already, clean out your water garden.

Remove dead flowers from plants growing in tubs, window-boxes and hanging baskets. Deadheading encourages more flowering and keeps displays looking tidy.

JUNE

8

9

Prune early-flowering shrubs and perennials when they are finished blooming.

10

11

Identify the insects you find in your garden. You may be surprised to find out how many are beneficial.

12

13

14

Despite the delicate look of its satiny flowers, godetia (*left*) thrives in poor soil and tolerates drought conditions.

Clockwise from top right: monarda; black-eyed Susans mixed with purple cone-flower; purple coneflower; artemisia; catmint

Perennials to pinch back in June:
- Artemisia (*Artemisia* species)
- Bee Balm (*Monarda didyma*)
- Black-eyed Susan (*Rudbeckia* species)
- Catmint (*Nepeta* hybrids)
- Purple Coneflower (*Echinacea purpurea*)
- Shasta Daisy (*Leucanthemum* hybrids)

JUNE

15

16

Pull weeds out of beds when you see them to avoid having to spend an entire day doing it later.

17

18

Water transplants regularly until they become established.

19

20

21

Coreopsis (*left*) enlivens a summer garden with its bright yellow, continuous blooms. Shear back in late summer for more flowers in fall.

Clockwise from top right: abutilon in a container; charming container garden display; million bells with bidens

CONTAINER GARDENING

Most plants can be grown in containers. Annuals, perennials, vegetables, shrubs and even trees can be adapted to container culture.

There are many advantages to gardening in containers:

- They work well in small spaces. Even apartment dwellers with small balconies can enjoy the pleasures of gardening with planters on the balcony.

- They are mobile. Containers can be moved around to take advantage of light or shade and can even be moved into a sheltered location for winter.

- They are easier to reach. Container plantings allow people in wheelchairs or with back problems to garden without having to do a lot of bending.

- They are useful for extending the season. Many plants require a longer growing season than we experience on the prairies. You can get an early start without the transplant shock that many plants suffer when moved outdoors.

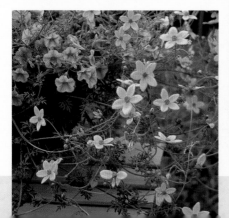

22

23

*Put trailing plants near the edge of
a container to spill out and bushy and upright
plants in the middle where they will give height
and depth to the planting.*

24

25

*Consider mixing different plants together in
a container. You can create contrasts of
colour, texture and habit and give a small
garden an inviting appearance.*

26

27

28

The flowers of *Salvia farinacea* 'Victoria' (*left*) are a
beautiful deep violet blue. They look stunning planted
with yellow or orange flowers such as nasturtiums,
California poppies or marigolds.

Clockwise from top right: a sensational array of annuals
in terra cotta pots; a deck improved by the presence of
a lush, vibrant container garden; tuberous begonias
mixed with million bells and trailing vinca

Gardeners can get more than a month's head start on the gardening season by using containers. Tomatoes, pumpkins and watermelons can be started from seed in April. Planted in large containers, they can be moved outside during warm days and brought back in at night for most of May. Doing so prevents the stretching that many early-started plants suffer from if kept indoors for too long before being planted in the garden.

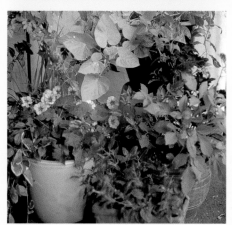

Many houseplants enjoy spending summer outside in a shady location. The brighter a location you provide for your plant indoors, the more likely it is to do well outdoors. Avoid putting plants in direct sun, though, because they will have a hard time adjusting to the intensity of the light and to the lack of light when they are moved back indoors at the end of summer.

JUNE

Keep an eye open for the early signs of pest and disease problems. They are easiest to deal with when they are just beginning.

Though considered old-fashioned by some gardeners, petunias (*below*) are versatile and dependable annuals that bloom continuously in any sunny location. New varieties of this flower seem to appear every spring in Alberta greenhouses.

Spirea (*top right*) by water feature

Water gardens can be created in containers. Many ready-made container gardens are available, or you can create your own. Garden centres have lots of water garden supplies, and many water plants will grow as well in a large tub as they will in a pond.

Most perennials, shrubs and trees will require more winter protection in containers than they would if grown in the ground. Because the roots are above ground level, they are exposed to the winter wind and cycles of freezing and thawing. Protect container-grown plants by insulating the inside of the container. Sheets of foam insulation can be purchased and fit around the inside of the pot before the soil is added. Containers can also be moved to sheltered locations. Garden sheds and unheated garages work well to protect plants from the cold and wind of winter.

Evergreens can be pruned once the new growth has fully extended, but while it is still tender. This new growth is called a 'candle' (*right*). Each can be pinched back by up to half to encourage bushier growth. Never cut evergreens back into old wood because most cannot regenerate from old wood.

JULY

The hot, sunny days of July encourage us
to sit back, relax and enjoy all the hard work
we've put into our gardens.

JULY

1

2

Deadhead repeat-blooming annuals and perennials regularly to keep them looking their best.

3

4

Cut flowers to use in fresh arrangements indoors.

5

6

7

The tender rose 'Ainsley Dickson' (*left*) is a reliable repeat bloomer in late summer if planted in full sun. It can produce up to 120 blossoms in its first season.

A riot of phlox, daylilies, yarrow, blue sage and snapdragons (*top right*); a natural-looking water feature (*bottom right*)

Flowerbeds have filled in, green tomatoes begin to ripen on the vine and the season's transplants are established and need less frequent watering.

With Alberta's long, warm days and short, cool nights, it sometimes seems as though you can watch your plants grow before your eyes. Gardeners from places with longer growing seasons are often amazed at how well things grow here. Never underestimate the power of extended growing days.

THINGS TO DO

Heat and drought can spell disaster for your lawn and garden if you haven't followed good watering practices. Water bans are common in communities all across Canada, and frequent, shallow watering earlier in the season makes for problems in July when roots unaccustomed to searching deeply for water suffer in its absence.

Water deeply, but no more than once a week during dry spells. Water early in the day to minimize potential disease and reduce water lost through evaporation.

Top up water gardens regularly if levels drop because of evaporation.

Thin vegetable crops such as beets, carrots and turnips. Crowded plants lead to poor crops.

JULY

8

9

Weed regularly to keep beds tidy.

10

11

Turn the compost pile and when the compost is ready, add it to your flowerbeds and vegetable garden.

12

13

14

Salvia (*left*) loves sun, and its brilliantly coloured flowers attract butterflies and hummingbirds to the garden. Plant it among other sun-loving annuals and perennials where its bright reds, oranges, pinks and purples will provide bright bursts of colour.

Clockwise from top right: violas; statice; bachelor's buttons

❧
Use an organic liquid fertilizer on container plants and on garden plants if compost is scarce.

❧
Pick zucchini when they are small. They are tender and tasty and you are less likely to wind up with boxes full of foot-long zucchini to leave on unsuspecting neighbours' front doorsteps. Consider donating extra vegetables to a homeless shelter or food bank, where they will be much appreciated.

Plan to replace fading flowers and vegetables by sowing seeds for a fall display or crop. Peas, bush beans, annual candytuft and lobelia are often finished fruiting or blooming by mid- to late summer, leaving holes in the garden that can be filled by new plants. Seeds for replacement plants can be direct sown or started indoors.

JULY

15

16

Top up mulch if it gets thin in places in your garden. Mulch protects roots and helps keep weeds at bay.

17

18

Continue to tie plants to their stakes as they grow.

19

20

Heliopsis (*left*), a native prairie perennial, is easy to grow and tolerates poor conditions, though it thrives in full sun and fertile, moist soil. Its name means 'resembling the sun' and its sun-like blooms make long-lasting cut flowers.

Use a mixture of annuals and perennials to create garden rooms that add privacy (*mid and bottom right*) or create paths through the garden (*far right*).

21

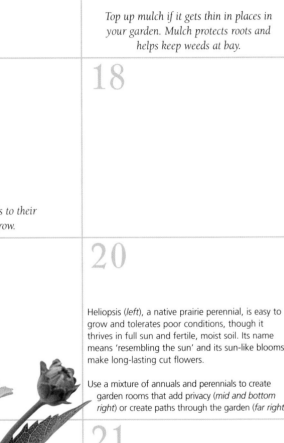

An important factor in ensuring the survival of a plant in your garden is where you plant it. Find out what the best growing conditions are for it to thrive, then put the plant where these conditions exist in your yard. A plant that needs full sun will never do well by your north-facing front door.

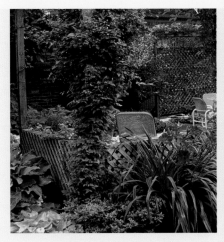

GARDEN PROBLEMS

Problems such as chewed leaves, mildews and nutrient deficiencies tend to become noticeable in July when plants finish their first flush of growth and turn their attention to flowering and fruiting.

Such problems can be minimized if you develop a good problem management program. Though it may seem complicated, problem management is a simple process that relies on correct and timely identification of the problem and then using the least environmentally harmful method to deal with it.

22

23

Prune shrubs that have finished flowering to encourage the development of young shoots that will bear flowers the following year.

24

25

Trim hedges regularly to keep them looking tidy and lush.

26

27

'Cupcake' (*left*) is a delightful miniature rose with a classic hybrid tea shape. It produces an abundance of blooms and is disease resistant.

Clockwise from top right: deer-pruned cedars; a swallowtail on cherry blossoms; a birdbath in a shade garden

28

Garden problems fall into three basic categories:

- pests, including insects such as aphids, nematodes and whiteflies, and animals such as mice, rabbits and deer
- diseases, caused by bacteria, fungi and viruses
- physiological problems, caused by nutrient deficiencies, too much or too little water and incorrect light levels.

Choose healthy plants that have been developed for their resistance to common problems and that will perform well in the conditions provided by your garden.

Prevention is the most important aspect of problem management. A healthy garden is resistant to problems and develops a natural balance between beneficial and detrimental organisms.

JULY

The natural pesticide pyrethrin is derived from certain species of chrysanthemums.

Cup-and-saucer vine (*below*) produces sweetly scented flowers that are cream coloured when they emerge and turn purple as they age.

Ladybug (*top right*), a beneficial insect that feasts on aphids; Dahlberg daisies (*bottom right*)

PEST CONTROL

Correct identification of problems is the key to solving them. Just because an insect is on a plant doesn't mean it's doing any harm.

Chemical pest control should always be a last resort. There are many alternatives that pose no danger to gardeners or their families and pets.

- Cultural controls are the day-to-day gardening techniques you use to keep your garden healthy. Weeding, mulching, keeping tools clean and growing problem-resistant cultivars are a few techniques you can use to keep gardens healthy.

- Physical controls are the hands-on part of problem solving. Picking insects off leaves, removing diseased foliage and creating barriers to stop rabbits from getting into the vegetable patch are examples of physical controls.

- Biological controls use natural and introduced populations of predators that prey on pests. Birds, snakes, frogs, spiders, some insects and even bacteria naturally feed on some problem insects. Soil microbes work with plant roots to increase their resistance to disease.

The pesticide industry has responded to consumer demand for effective, environmentally safe pest control products. Biopesticides are made from plant, animal, bacterial or mineral sources. They are effective in small quantities and decompose quickly in the environment. These products may reduce our reliance on chemical pesticides.

AUGUST

Though the warm weather continues,
the ripening fruit, vegetables and seeds are
signs that summer is nearing its end.

1

2

Reduce fertilizer applications to allow perennials, shrubs and trees ample time to harden off before the cold weather.

3

4

Continue to water during dry spells. Plants shouldn't need deep watering more than once a week at this time of the year.

5

6

7

Calendula (*left*) is an easy flower to grow from seed. It blooms quickly in spring and all summer long, even tolerating light frost. It can be used as a culinary herb as well.

Clockwise from top right: borage; deadheading asters; petunias.

The nights are getting longer and cooler, and a few trees may even begin to colour, indicators of the approaching days of fall. A frost is possible, but not common, in August.

THINGS TO DO

The garden seems to take care of itself in August. We gardeners putter about, tying up floppy hollyhock spikes, picking vegetables and pulling an odd weed, but the frenzy of early summer is over and we take the time just to sit and enjoy the results of our labours.

Continue to deadhead perennials and annuals to keep the blooms coming.

Remove worn-out annuals and vegetables, and replace them with the ones you started last month. Shearing some annuals and perennials back will encourage new growth, giving them a fresh look for fall.

Keep an eye open for pests that may be planning to hibernate in the debris around your plants or the bark of your trees. Taking care of a few insects now may keep several generations out of your garden next summer.

Pick apples as soon as they are ready, being careful not to bruise the fruit.

8

9

*Seed areas of lawn that are thin or dead.
The cool weather encourages fast growth. Keep
the seed well watered while it germinates.*

10

11

*Depending on the size of your perennials,
you can divide them using a shovel or
pitchfork (for large plants), a sharp knife
(for small plants) or your hands
(for easily divided plants).*

12

13

14

The French marigold (*left*) is just
one variety of this popular
annual. All marigolds are low-
maintenance plants that stand up
well to heat, wind and rain.

PLANT PROPAGATION

Now is a good time to divide some perennials and to note which of your plants will need dividing next spring. Look for these signs that perennials need dividing:

- The centre of the plant has died out.
- The plant is no longer flowering as profusely as it did in previous years.
- The plant is encroaching on the growing space of other plants.

August is a good time to propagate plants. Taking cuttings and gathering seed are great ways to increase your plant collection and to share some of your favourite plants with friends and family.

Prairie-hardy species such as Siberian bugloss (*top*), anenome (*top right*), liatrus (*centre*) and penstemon (*right*) are good plants to divide if you're just starting your perennial collection. All are drought tolerant, especially important on the often-dry prairies.

15

16

Gradually move houseplants that have been summering outdoors into shadier locations so they will be prepared for the lower light levels indoors. Make sure they aren't infested with bugs; the pests will be harder to control once the plants are indoors.

17

18

Turn the layers of the compost pile and continue to add garden soil, kitchen scraps and garden debris that isn't diseased or infested with insects.

19

20

Zinnias (*below*) are easy to grow, come in a rainbow of colours and make long-lasting cut flowers for floral arrangements.

Clockwise from top right: basket-of-gold, sedum and aster are easy to propagate from stem cuttings.

21

Perennials, trees, shrubs and tender perennials that are treated like annuals can all be started from cuttings. This method is an excellent way to propagate varieties and cultivars that you really like but that are slow or difficult to start from seed or that don't produce viable seed.

The easiest cuttings to take from woody plants such as trees, shrubs and vines are called semi-ripe, semi-mature or semi-hardwood cuttings. They are taken from mature new growth that has not become completely woody yet, usually in late summer or early fall.

There is some debate over what size cuttings should be. Some claim that smaller cuttings are more likely to root and will root more quickly. Others claim that larger cuttings develop more roots and become established more quickly once planted. Try different sizes and see what works best for you.

AUGUST

22

23

Continue watering newly planted perennials, trees and shrubs. Water deeply to encourage root growth.

24

25

Avoid pruning rust-prone plants such as mountain ash and crabapple in late summer and fall because many rusts are releasing spores now.

26

27

28

Start collecting seeds from your borage plants (*left*) in August for planting next season.

Clockwise from top right: evening primrose; nasturtiums with creeping Jenny; zinnias

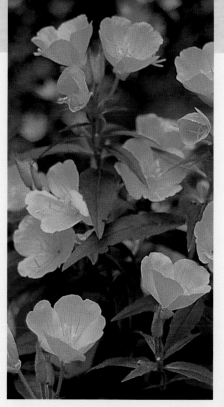

The easiest way to start is to collect seeds of annual plants in your own garden. Choose plants that are not hybrids or the seeds will probably not come true to type and may not germinate at all. A few easy plants to collect from are

- Borage (*Borago officinalis*)
- Calendula (*Calendula officinalis*)
- Coriander (*Coriandrum sativum*)
- Evening Primrose (*Oenothera fruticosa*)
- Fennel (*Foeniculum vulgare*)
- Marigold (*Tagetes* species and hybrids)
- Nasturtium (*Tropaeolum majus*)
- Poppy (*Papaver rhoeas*)
- Zinnia (*Zinnia elegans*)

Always make cuttings just below a leaf node, the point where the leaves are attached to the stem.

Many gardeners enjoy the hobby of collecting and planting seed. You need to know a few basic things before you begin:

- Know your plant. Correctly identify the plant and learn about its life cycle. You will need to know when it flowers, when the seeds are likely to ripen and how the plant disperses its seeds in order to collect them.
- Find out if there are special requirements for starting the seeds. For example, do they need a hot or cold period to germinate?

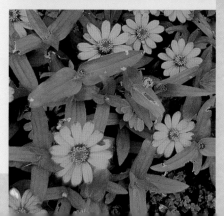

29

30

*Find a source of straw for mulch
now because it can be harder
to find later in fall.*

31

Nasturtiums (*below*) are versatile annuals. Their edible flowers and foliage are attractive additions to baskets and containers as well as to salads. Even the seedpods can be pickled and used as a substitute for capers.

Clockwise from top right: drying poppy seedheads; Oriental poppy; golden clematis flowers and seedheads

When collecting seed, consider the following:

- Collect seeds once they are ripe but before they are shed from the parent plant.

- Remove capsules, heads or pods as they begin to dry and remove the seeds later, once they are completely dry.

- Place a paper bag over a seed-head as it matures and loosely tie it in place to collect seeds as they are shed.

- Dry seeds after they've been collected. Place them on a paper-lined tray and leave them in a warm, dry location for one to three weeks.

- Separate seeds from the other plant parts before storing.

- Store seeds in air-tight containers in a cool, frost-free location.

Don't collect seeds from the wild because wild harvesting is severly depleting many plant populations. Many species and populations of wild plants are protected, and it is illegal to collect their seeds.

Collecting and saving seeds is a time-honoured tradition. Early settlers brought seeds with them when they came here and saved them carefully each fall for the following spring.

September

Though we cling tenaciously to any summer weather that lingers, there's no denying that fall is upon us.

SEPTEMBER

1

2

*Pull out annual plants and vegetables
as they fade or are killed by frost.*

3

4

*Plant colourful fall ornamentals, such
as chrysanthemums, flowering cabbage
and flowering kale, available in
fall at most garden centres.*

5

6

7

Goldenrod (*left*), amaranthus (*top right*), strawflower
(*centre right*) and nigella (*bottom right*) can be harvested now for dried flower arrangements.

Leaves are changing colour, ripening seedheads nod in the breeze and brightly coloured berries and fruit adorn many trees and shrubs. There is a strong likelihood of frost before the end of September, particularly in areas outside the limits of the larger cities. Many annuals will continue undamaged by early frosts and bloom until the first hard freeze.

THINGS TO DO

Having enjoyed another summer garden, your big fall clean-up begins.

Take advantage of end-of-season sales. Many garden centres are getting rid of trees, shrubs and perennials at reduced prices. There is still plenty of time for the roots to become established before the ground freezes. Do not buy plants that are excessively pot bound.

Consider starting some herb seeds now. You can plant them in pots and keep them in a bright window so you'll have fresh herbs to add to soups and salads over winter. Moving herb plants in from outdoors is also possible, but the plants often have a difficult time adapting to the lower light levels indoors.

SEPTEMBER

8

9

Dig up tuberous tender plants such as begonias for drying and storing over winter.

10

11

Continue to water the garden during dry spells. Consistent watering in fall helps prepare plants for winter.

12

13

Lilies (*left*) are long-lived, easy-to-grow perennials. They look superb in floral arrangements combined with flowers such as baby's breath (*left*).

Clockwise from top right: the fall colours and features of Virginia creeper, burning bush, viburnum (highbush cranberry) and horse chestnut

14

If you've let your weeds get out of hand over summer, be sure to pull them up before they set seed to avoid having even more weeds popping up in the garden next summer.

Cool fall weather is ideal for sowing grass seed and repairing thin patches in the lawn.

So many trees and shrubs in Alberta turn shades of yellow, gold and orange in the fall that it really turns our heads when we see a brilliant red. A good selection of hardy plants consistently turns bright red in fall. A few examples are

- Amur Maple (*Acer ginnala*)
- Burning Bush (*Euonymus alatus*)
- Highbush Cranberry (*Viburnum trilobum*)
- Virginia Creeper (*Parthenocissus quinquefolia*)
- Peking Cotoneaster (*Cotoneaster lucidus*)

SEPTEMBER

15

16

Set up birdfeeders and begin to feed
the birds if you didn't do so all summer.

17

18

Move tender container plants into a
sheltered location when frost is
expected. This strategy will allow you
to enjoy them for longer.

19

20

The cheery golden marguerite daisy plant (*below*)
forms a tidy mound that works wonderfully in both
formal and informal garden settings.

Clockwise from top right: primroses; tulips with candy-
tuft; *alliums*; rudbeckia (black-eyed Susan)

21

Begin to plant bulbs for a great display next spring. Tulips, daffodils, crocuses, scillas, muscaris and alliums are just a few of the bulbs whose flowers will welcome you back into the garden next year.

Spring-flowering perennials such as primroses and candy-tuft will be a delightful sight come April and May.

For vivacious colour from summer through fall, a continuous blooming perennial such as rudbeckia can't be beat.

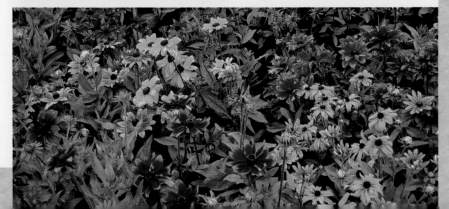

SEPTEMBER

22

23

When planting bulbs, don't forget to add a little bonemeal to the soil to encourage root development.

24

25

Check houseplants for insect pests before moving them back indoors for winter.

26

27

Echinacea purpurea (*left*), commonly called purple coneflower and used as a popular herbal cold remedy, is a long-blooming, drought-resistant perennial. Its distinctively cone-shaped flowers look good in fresh and dried floral arrangements.

Opposite page: Garden features such as birdbaths, bird feeders and tall flowering perennials such as beebalm, coneflower and yarrow attract wildlife to your yard.

28

CREATING WILDLIFE HABITAT

The rapid rate of urban sprawl has led to the relentless expansion of large cities and a loss of habitat for wildlife. Our gardens can easily provide some of the space, shelter, food and water that wildlife needs. Though we may not want to attract every creature, we can make at least some wildlife welcome in our gardens. Here are a few tips for attracting wildlife to your garden:

- Make sure at least some of the plants in your garden are locally native. Birds and small animals are accustomed to certain plants for food. These plants will attract the wildlife to your garden, where it may be tempted to try some of the other fruit that is not native.

- Provide a source of water. A pond with a shallow side or a birdbath will offer water for drinking and bathing. Frogs and toads eat a wide variety of insect pests and will happily take up residence in or near a ground-level water feature.

- A variety of birdfeeders and seed will encourage different species of birds to visit your garden. Some birds will visit an elevated feeder, but others prefer a feeder set at or near ground level. Fill your feeders regularly—once you start to feed the birds, they will come to depend on you as a source of food.

SEPTEMBER

The zinnia (*below*) is named after Johann Gottfried Zinn (1727–59), a German botany professor who first grew a South American zinnia from seed.

Clockwise from top right: birdfeeder; monarda with butterfly; sunflower; maple tree

- Butterflies, hummingbirds and a wide variety of predatory insects will be attracted if you include lots of pollen-producing plants in your garden. Plants such as goldenrod, comfrey, bee balm, salvia, Joe-Pye weed, black-eyed Susan, catmint, purple coneflower, coreopsis, hollyhock and yarrow will attract pollen lovers.

- Shelter is the final aspect to keeping your resident wildlife happy. Patches of dense shrubs, tall grasses and mature trees provide shelter. As well, you can leave a small pile of twiggy brush in an out-of-the-way place. Nature stores and many garden centres sell toad houses and birdhouses.

Inevitably squirrels and chipmunks will try to get at your birdfeeders. In areas where squirrels are not a problem, instead of trying to get rid of them, why not leave peanuts and seeds out for them as well? Place them near a tree, where they can easily get at them. If you have a large spruce tree, they will eat the seeds out of the cones. Leave cones out with the other food offerings. The little cone scales that are left when they are done make great mulch for the garden or can be used to prevent slipping on icy walks and driveways.

OCTOBER

This month marks the inevitable end of summer. Only a few hardy bloomers may still be going strong by month's end.

OCTOBER

1

2

Continue to plant bulbs. They need to get a bit of root growth in fall in order to survive winter.

3

4

Continue to mow the lawn, but don't mow frozen blades of grass. Wait for frost to melt off and dry before cutting the grass.

5

6

If the first frost hasn't yet arrived and your apples are still on the tree (*left*), now is the time to harvest them. However, some varieties taste better after the first frost.

Clockwise from top right: fall wreath made from garden clippings; a bountiful harvest of carrots; endearing teddy bear sunflowers

7

Octover lawns and leaves are dusted with frost in the mornings and even an occasional early snowfall. We enjoy any warm spell all the more because we know how cold it will be soon.

THINGS TO DO

October is the time to finish tidying up and putting the garden to bed for another year.

Harvest any remaining vegetables. Soft fruit such as tomatoes and zucchini should have been harvested before the first frost, but cool-weather vegetables such as carrots, cabbage, brussels sprouts, parsnips and turnips can wait until October because they are frost hardy.

Unless your plants have been afflicted with some sort of disease, you can leave faded perennial growth in place and clean it up in spring. The stems will collect leaves and snow, protecting the roots and crown of the plant over the winter.

OCTOBER

8

9

Continue to tidy up dead plant material. Most can be composted, but diseased material is better thrown out.

10

11

Start mulching the garden, but avoid covering plants completely until the ground has frozen. Doing so prevents plants from rotting and deters small rodents from digging down and feasting on plant roots and crowns.

12

13

14

The leaves of the evergreen groundcover kinnikinnick (*left*), a plant native to Alberta, turn a lovely bronze-red in fall. The berries are a source of food for birds and other wildlife.

Fall is a great time to improve your soil. Amendments added now can be worked in lightly. By planting time next spring, the amendments will have been further worked in by the actions of worms and other soil microorganisms and by the freezing and thawing that takes place over winter.

When raking up leaves in fall, you can use them in different ways: add them to the compost pile; gather them into their own compost pile to decompose into leaf mould; or mow them over and then pile them onto flowerbeds. Whole leaves can become matted together, encouraging fungal rot.

Local farmers' markets are often the best places to find a wide variety of seasonal vegetables and flowers (*above and below*).

OCTOBER

16

Continue to water trees and shrubs until freeze up. Apply an organic anti-desiccant to newly planted shrubs and evergreens for added winter protection.

After raking, and once the lawn is dormant, apply an organic fertilizer. If you haven't needed to mow in a couple of weeks, it is probably sufficiently dormant.

Honeysuckle vine (*left*) flowers from summer to fall frost. Prune in spring to cut back dead growth as new leaves emerge.

Composting (*far right*); delicious vegetables harvested from the garden (*near right*)

COMPOSTING

One of the best additives for any type of soil is compost. Compost can be purchased at most garden centres, and many communities now have composting programs. You can easily make compost in your own garden. Though garden refuse and vegetable scraps from your kitchen left in a pile will eventually decompose, it is possible to produce compost more quickly. Here are a few suggestions for creating compost:

■ Compost decomposes most quickly when there is a balance between dry and fresh materials. There should be more dry matter, such as chopped straw or shredded leaves, than green matter, such as vegetable scraps and grass clippings.

■ Layer the dry and the green matter and mix in some garden soil or previously finished compost. This step introduces decomposer organisms to the pile.

22

23

As outdoor gardening winds down,
try starting bulbs such as paperwhites
(narcissus) indoors. Fragrant white blooms
should emerge in a few weeks.

24

25

Cure winter squash, such as pumpkins,
acorn squash and spaghetti squash,
in a cool, frost-free location before
storing for winter.

26

27

28

Yarrow's showy, flat-topped flowerheads (*left*) provide months of continuous colour in summer and persist into
winter.

■ Compost won't decompose properly if it is too wet or too dry. Keep the pile covered during heavy rain and sprinkle it with water if it is too dry. The correct level of moisture can best be described as that of a wrung-out sponge.

■ To aerate the pile, use a garden fork to poke holes in it or turn it regularly. Use a thermometer with a long probe attached, similar to a large meat thermometer, to check the temperature in your pile. When the temperature drops, give the pile a turn.

■ Finished compost is dark in colour and light in texture. When you can no longer recognize what went into the compost, it is ready for use.

■ Compost can be mixed into garden soil or spread on the surface as a mulch.

Images of fall: the ripening berries of the viburnum (*top left*); juicy clusters of vine-ripened grapes (*top*); tasty corn on the cob fresh from the garden (*above*). Though many people assume grapes won't grow in Alberta, numerous varieties are available for eating and wine and juice making.

OCTOBER

29

30

If you haven't got the time or the inclination to fuss over your compost, you can just leave it in a pile and it will eventually decompose with no added assistance from you.

31

Sunflowers (*below*) are synonymous with fall for many gardeners. Their bold yellow, seed-filled flowerheads celebrate the harvest season and provide treats for the birds.

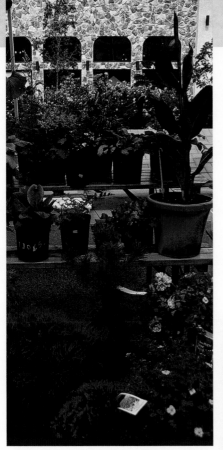

Before adding any amendments to your soil, you should get a soil test done. Simple kits to test for pH and major nutrients are available at garden centres. More thorough tests are done at government or private labs. These tests will tell you what the pH is, the comparative levels of sand, silt, clay and organic matter and the quantities of all required nutrients. They will also tell you what amendments to add and in what quantities to improve your soil.

There are other good amendments for soil, depending on what is required:

- Gypsum can be mixed into a clay soil along with compost to loosen the structure and allow water to penetrate.
- Elemental sulphur, peat moss or pine needles added on a regular basis can make an alkaline soil more acidic.
- Calcitic or dolomitic limestone, hydrated lime, quicklime or wood ashes can be added to an acidic soil to make it more alkaline.

Sunflowers (*above*) and other cut flowers can be found in abundance in farmers' markets (*top left*) throughout the province. Use them for fresh or dried table arrangements, or flower pressing for winter crafts.

NOVEMBER

November often marks the beginning of winter in Alberta. We start to forget this year's garden and turn our thoughts to next summer.

NOVEMBER

1

2

Faded annuals and vegetables can be pulled up and added to the compost pile.

3

4

If you have healthy willows, dogwoods, Virginia creeper or evergreens, cut a few branches to use in Christmas wreaths. Store in a cool place until needed.

5

6

7

Annual coreopsis (*left*) self-seeds, so it may pop up from year to year in the same area if left to its own devices.

Despite the inevitable frosts, a few stragglers always hang on. Flowers such as calendula keep blooming, even under a light blanket of snow, until the ground starts to freeze. The ground may freeze by mid-month, but some years it doesn't until December.

THINGS TO DO

Garden tasks this month centre around finishing tucking the garden in for winter.

Harvest any remaining vegetables. Root vegetables, such as carrots, parsnips and turnips, and green vegetables, such as cabbages and broccoli, store well in a cool place, and their flavour is often improved after a touch of frost.

The garden can be quite beautiful in November, especially with a light dusting of snow on branches with persistent fruits (*right, below*).

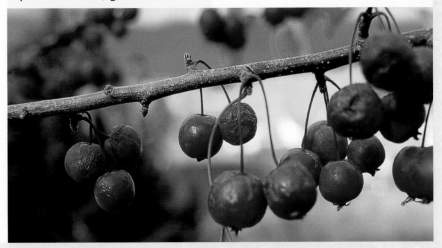

NOVEMBER

8

9

Clear away tools, hoses and garden furniture before the snow flies so they won't be damaged by the cold and wet weather.

10

11

Mound mulch around the bases of semi-hardy shrubs to protect the roots and stem bases from temperature fluctuations.

12

13

The richly coloured rosettes of ornamental kale (*far right, centre right* and *bottom right*), which often persists into November, are reminiscent of roses (*top right*), particularly the long-stemmed, small-headed varieties.

14

The beautiful hybrid tea rose 'Rosemary Harkness' (*left*) produces fragrant orange-yellow double blooms from summer to autumn. Like other tender hybrid teas, it should be protected from Alberta's harsh winter weather.

Prepare hybrid tea and other semi-hardy roses for winter early in the month. Mound dirt over the base of the rose and cover with mulch, or cover it with a cardboard box, open the top and fill around the plant with loose, quick-drying material, such as sawdust, shredded leaves or peat moss. Hold the box in place with a heavy rock on top when you are done.

Avoid completely covering perennials with mulch until the ground freezes. Mound the mulch around them, and store some extra mulch in a frost-free location to add once they are frozen. If you pile the mulch in the garden, you may find it has also frozen solid when you want to use it.

15

16

*Be sure to enjoy any remaining
warm days before the garden becomes
the dream of next summer.*

17

18

*Fill your birdfeeders regularly.
Well-fed birds will continue to visit your
garden in summer, feeding on undesirable
insects in your garden.*

19

20

21

Ornamental kale (*left*) is one of the most frost-hardy annuals; its colours actually intensify as fall temperatures drop. When planted en masse in flowerbeds, it creates stunning patterns.

Clockwise from top right: hollyhock; hens and chicks; jack pine; peashrub (caragana)

If an area of your garden always seems dry, consider a xeriscape planting in that area. Many plants are drought resistant and thrive even in areas that are never watered. Yarrow, hollyhock, prickly pear cactus, black-eyed Susan, jack pine, potentilla, peashrub and cosmos are just a few of the many possibilities for a dry section of the garden.

Now that you've had the chance to observe your garden for a growing season, consider the microclimates and think about how you can put them to good use. Are any always quick to dry? Do some areas stay wet longer than others? What area is the most sheltered? Which is the least sheltered? Cater your plantings to the microclimates of your garden.

NOVEMBER

22

23

*Wait for the ground to freeze up before
covering or wrapping tender shrubs
and evergreens to ensure that all growth
has slowed for winter.*

24

25

*Spray anti-desiccants on evergreens, such as
rhododendrons and cedars, to prevent
moisture loss over winter.*

26

27

28

Flowers such as marsh marigolds (*left*), irises (*top
and far right*), daylilies (*centre right*) and ligularia
(*bottom right*) work well in damp areas of the garden because they prefer moist growing conditions.

BOG GARDENING

Turn a damp area into your own little bog garden. Dig out a damp area 35–50 cm (14–20") below ground level, line with a piece of punctured pond liner and fill with soil. The area will stay wet but still allow some water to drain away, providing a perfect location to plant moisture-loving perennials. A few to consider are

- Astilbe (*Astilbe* x *arendsii*)
- Daylily (*Hemerocallis* hybrids)
- Doronicum (*Doronicum orientale*)
- Goatsbeard (*Aruncus dioicus*)
- Hosta (*Hosta* hybrids)
- Iris (*Iris ensata, Iris siberica*)
- Lady's Mantle (*Alchemilla mollis*)
- Ligularia (*Ligularia dentata* and *wilsoniana*)
- Lily-of-the-Valley (*Convallaria majalis*)
- Marsh Marigold (*Caltha palustris*)
- Meadowsweet (*Filipendula rubra* and *ulmaria*)
- Primrose (*Primula japonica*)
- Rodgersia (*Rodgersia aesculifolia*)

Finish collecting seeds from open-pollinated flowers and vegetables. Stored in a cool, dry place, they will be ready for planting in next year's garden.

Rodgersia (*left*) bears bold foliage and fluffy flower plumes in mid- to late summer. It does best in a site sheltered from strong winds and extreme weather. Rodgersia plants prefer moist soil and require winter protection in Alberta.

Plants that will need some winter protection in Alberta, *clockwise from top right*: gingko displaying fall colour; star magnolia; gingko leaves in spring; azalea

The warmest, most sheltered area
of your garden should be reserved
for those plants that are not fully
hardy here in the chilly north.
Azalea, star magnolia and ginko are
just a few of the many out of zone
plants that have proven themselves
capable of withstanding our cold
winters if planted in a suitably
sheltered location.

If you have a very exposed area in
your garden, you can find plants
that will do well there, or you can
make a planting that will shelter
the area. A cotoneaster hedge or
group planting will break the wind
and provide an attractive feature
for your garden.

DECEMBER

*Already summer seems far away. Ghostly
forms and dashes of colour are all that
remain to inspire us until spring.*

DECEMBER

1

2

If you haven't already done so, finish mulching the garden.

3

4

Clean tools thoroughly and wipe them with an oily rag to prevent them from rusting before storing them for winter.

5

6

7

Holly (*left*) makes an attractive addition to fresh winter arrangements. To keep it looking its best, keep the cut ends consistently moist.

The garden begins its winter display of colourful, peeling bark, branches with persistent fruit and evergreen boughs. Snow piles up on garden beds, covering withered perennials and shrubs and clinging to evergreen branches. Winter arrives, often with a vengeance, driving away our fond memories of the garden.

THINGS TO DO

Our thoughts turn to indoor gardening though we may still have a few garden tasks to complete before we call it a year.

Gently brush snow off flexible evergreen branches. Heavy snow can weigh down upright juniper and cedar branches enough to permanently bend them downwards.

Water evergreens and shrubs thoroughly before the ground freezes. They won't have any access to water again until the ground thaws in spring.

If rabbits and mice are a problem in your garden, you can protect your trees and shrubs with chicken wire. Wrap it around the plant bases and higher up the tree or shrub than you expect the snow to reach.

In December our thoughts turn to decorating for the holidays. Now is the time to use some of the flowers you dried to make potpourri, wreaths or floral arrangements (*above and left*).

DECEMBER

8

9

Move clay and concrete pots and statues into a protected location to prevent them from cracking over winter.

10

11

Chinese evergreen, Easter cactus, Norfolk Island pine, peacock plant, peace lily and prayer plant are some houseplants that tolerate low light levels.

12

13

14

Poinsettias (*left*) add rich colour and beauty to our homes during the dark days of December.

Clockwise from top right: ficus (weeping fig); *Cattleya* orchid; *Miltonopsis* orchid; cast iron plant

HOUSEPLANT CARE

You don't have to forget gardening completely when the snow begins to fly. All you have to do is turn your attention to indoor gardening. Houseplants clean the air, soften the hard edges of a room and provide colour, texture and interest to your home.

Just as you did for the garden outdoors, match your indoor plants to the conditions your home provides. If a room receives little light, consider houseplants that require low light levels. Plants that like humid conditions, such as African violets, ferns and philodendrons, may do best in your bathroom, where water from showering and the toilet bowl maintain higher moisture levels than in any other room. Plants that tolerate or prefer dry air, such as cacti, ficus, palms and poinsettias, will grow well with no added humidity.

15

16

Most indoor plant pests can be controlled by wiping leaves with a damp sponge. More difficult pests can be controlled with insecticidal soap.

17

18

Bright-light tolerant plants include cacti, goldfish plant, jade plant and snake plant.

19

20

Although orchids are reputed to be difficult and needy, some orchids such as the moth orchid *Phalaenopsis (left)* are easy to grow on a windowsill. There are many thousands of species of orchids in an amazing array of sizes, shapes, colours and fragrances.

Indoor water garden (*centre right*); braided lucky bamboo (*bottom right*)

21

There are three aspects of interior light to consider: intensity, duration and quality. Intensity is the difference between a south-facing window with full sun and a north-facing room with no direct sunlight. Duration is how long the light lasts in a specific location. An east-facing window will have a shorter duration of light than a south-facing window. Quality refers to the spectrum of the light. Natural light provides a broader spectrum than artificial light.

Watering is a key element to houseplant care. Over-watering can be as much of a problem as under-watering. As you did with your garden plants, water thoroughly and infrequently. Let the soil dry out a bit before watering plants. Some plants are the exception to this rule. Find out what the water requirements of your houseplants are so you will have an idea of how frequently or infrequently you will need to water.

Look for creative ways to display your plants and add humidity to your home. Indoor fountains and moisture-loving plants, such as a peace lily, in a vase of water (*top*), adds much-needed moisture to your home during the dry winter months.

22

23

*Dust on plants is more than just an eyesore.
It prevents plants from making full use
of the light they receive. Clean leaves
regularly with a damp cloth or sponge
or place them in the shower and let
the water stream wash away any dust.*

24

25

26

27

28

English ivy (*left*) that you've grown outdoors all summer can be brought indoors and kept as a houseplant in winter.

An interesting houseplant display (*top right*); snake plant (*bottom right*), a striking, long-lived indoor plant

Houseplants generally only need fertilizer when they are actively growing. Always use a weak fertilizer to avoid burning the roots. Never feed plants when they are very dry. Moisten the soil by watering and then feed a couple of days later.

When repotting, go up by only one size at a time. In general the new pot should be no more than 5–10 cm (2–4") larger in diameter than the previous pot. If you find your soil drying out too frequently, then you may wish to use a larger pot that will stay moist for longer.

Houseplants are more than just attractive—they clean the air in our homes. Many dangerous and common toxins, such as benzene, formaldehyde and trichloroethylene are absorbed and eliminated by houseplants.

Here are a few easy-to-grow, toxin-absorbing houseplants:

- Spider Plant (*Chlorophytum cosmosum*)
- Peace Lily (*Spathiphyllum* 'Mauna Loa')
- Bamboo Palm (*Camaedorea erumpens*)
- Pot Mum (*Chrysanthemum morifolium*)
- English Ivy (*Hedera helix*)
- Weeping Fig (*Ficus benjamina*)
- Chinese Evergreen (*Aglaonema modestum*)
- Dragon Tree (*Dracaena marginata*)
- Snake Plant (*Sansevieria trifasciata*)
- Gerbera Daisy (*Gerbera jamesonii*)

DECEMBER

29

Plants can be grouped together in large containers to more easily meet the needs of the plants. Cacti can be planted together in a gritty soil mix and placed in a dry, bright location. Moisture and humidity-loving plants can be planted in a large terrarium where moisture levels remain higher.

30

31

A bouquet of cheerful gerberas (*below*) will brighten a drab winter day and remind you of summer, when these flowers were growing in your garden.

Cacti (*near right*) make good houseplants because they are undemanding and tolerate the dry air found in most Alberta homes quite well.

Keep in mind that many common houseplants are tropical and dislike hot, dry conditions. Most house-plants will thrive in cooler, moister conditions than you will provide in your home. Always turn thermo-stats down at night and provide moist conditions by sitting pots on pebble trays. Water in the pebble tray can evaporate but won't soak excessively into the soil of the pot because the pebbles hold it above the water.

There's nothing like treating yourself to a bouquet of fresh flowers (*above*) when you're feeling the doldrums of winter. Spring and fall-flowering varieties from the coast and California are widely available at grocery stores and florist shops. Watch for some of the more exotic plants from South America and Australia.

RESOURCES

Books

Brickell, C., T.J. Cole and J.D. Zuk, eds. 1996. *Reader's Digest A–Z Encyclopedia of Garden Plants*. The Reader's Digest Association Ltd., Montreal, PQ.

Brickell, C. and David Joyce. 1996. *Pruning and Training*. Dorling Kindersley Limited, London, England.

Bubel, Nancy. 1988. *The New Seed Starter's Handbook*. Rodale Press, Emmaus, PA.

The Calgary Horticultural Society. 1996. *The Calgary Gardener*. Fifth House, Calgary, AB.

Casselman, Bill. 1997. *Canadian Garden Words*. Little, Brown and Company (Canada) Ltd., Toronto, ON.

Courtier, Jane and Graham Clarke. 1997. *Indoor Plants: The Essential Guide to Choosing and Caring for Houseplants*. Reader's Digest, Westmount, PQ.

Ellis, B.W. and F.M. Bradley, eds. 1996. *The Organic Gardener's Handbook of Natural Insect and Disease Control*. Rodale Press, Emmaus, PA.

Flanagan, June and Donna Fremont. 2001. *The Prairie Gardener's Sourcebook*. Fifth House, Calgary, AB.

Heintzelman, Donald S. 2001. *The Complete Backyard Birdwatcher's Home Companion*. Ragged Mountain Press, Camden, ME.

Hole, Lois. 1993. *Lois Hole's Vegetable Favorites*. Lone Pine Publishing, Edmonton, AB.

— — —. 1994. *Lois Hole's Bedding Plant Favorites*. Lone Pine Publishing, Edmonton, AB.

— — —. 1995. *Lois Hole's Perennial Favorites*. Lone Pine Publishing, Edmonton, AB.

— — —. 1996. *Lois Hole's Tomato Favorites*. Lone Pine Publishing, Edmonton, AB.

— — —. 1997. *Lois Hole's Rose Favorites*. Lone Pine Publishing, Edmonton, AB.

— — —. 1997. *Lois Hole's Favorite Trees and Shrubs*. Lone Pine Publishing, Edmonton, AB.

Hill, Lewis. 1991. *Secrets of Plant Propagation*. Storey Communications Inc., Pownal, VT.

Knowles, Hugh. 1995. *Woody Ornamentals for the Prairies*. University of Alberta Press, Edmonton, AB.

Leatherbarrow, Liesbeth and Lesley Reynolds. 1999. *101 Best Plants for the Prairies*. Fifth House, Calgary, AB.

— — —. 2001. *Best Bulbs for the Prairies*. Fifth House, Calgary, AB.
McHoy, Peter. 2002. *Houseplants*. Hermes House, New York, NY.

McHoy, Peter. 2002. *Houseplants.* Hermes House, New York, NY.

McVicar, Jekka. 1997. *Jekka's Complete Herb Book.* Raincoast, Vancouver, BC.

Merilees, Bill. 1989. *Attracting Backyard Wildlife: A Guide for Nature Lovers.* Voyageur Press, Stillwater, MN.

Robinson, Peter. 1997. *Complete Guide to Water Gardening.* Reader's Digest, Westmount, PQ.

Thompson, P. 1992. *Creative Propagation: A Grower's Guide.* Timber Press, Portland, OR.

Online Resources

Alberta Agriculture. Ask the expert, and pests and diseases sections. www.agric.gov.ab.ca/

Attracting Wildlife to your garden.com. How to make your backyard inviting to compatible and beneficial creatures. www.attracting-wildlife-to-your-garden.com

Bedrock Seed Bank. Provides seed from over 630 varieties to enable gardeners to reestablish native varieties. www.albertadirectory.net/bedrockseed/

Canadian Gardening. Ask the expert section and an extensive listing of gardening catalogues. www.canadiangardening.com/home.html

Canadian Organic Advisory Board Inc. Information and resources for gardening organically across Canada. www.coab.ca, www.coab.ca/gardening.htm

Canadian Organic Growers. Information on organic growing. www.cog.ca

Composting Council of Canada. A national non-profit organization that encourages composting. www.compost.org

Devonian Botanic Garden. Gardening tips, seeds, books, ask the expert, Master Gardener program, upcoming events. www.discoveredmonton.com/devonian/

Evergreen Foundation. Provides tools to transform residential and commercial spaces into healthy outdoor spaces. www.evergreen.ca/en/index.html

Hollandia Flowers and Bulbs. 1-780-963-7307 or 1-780-963-8153 goosemeadow@hotmail.com (contact: Kevin Frey)

I Can Garden. Information and a gardening forum where you can contact gardeners from across Canada and the world. www.icangarden.com/

Northern Garden. List of Alberta plant and seed sources.www.connect.ab.ca/~buddy/seedsaba.html

Northern Gardening Forum. List of gardening forums intended for northern USA but used by many Canadians. www.northerngardening.com

Prairie Frontier. Create an easy-to-maintain landscape that is inviting to wildlife, butterflies and birds. www.prairiefrontier.com/pages/families/attracts.html

Seeds of Diversity Canada. Saves and shares seeds of rare, unusual and heritage plants. www.seeds.ca/en.htm

Sprout Farms. Order scion wood for grafting, or take a class in grafting and budding fruit stock. www.cw.interbaun.com/sprout/

Turf Resource Center and The Lawn Institute. The latest data regarding turfgrass. www.TurfGrassSod.org www.LawnInstitute.com

University of Illinois Extension. Information on houseplant care, annuals, perennials, growing vegetables and fruit, diseases and insects, herbs and seasonal features. www.urbanext.uiuc.edu/houseplants/

Soil-Testing Facilities
Midwest Laboratories Canada (soil, water, plants, feed, manure)
#8, 4001B–19th St., NE, Calgary, AB T2E 6X8
1–403–250–3317; fax: 1–403–250–5249
email: mwl@midwestlabscanada.com

Norwest Labs (soil, water, air nutrients)
Environmental & Agri-Food
9938–67 Ave., Edmonton, AB T6E 0P5
1–780–438–5522 or 1–800–661–7645

Bay 6, 2712–37th Ave., NE, Calgary, AB T1Y 5L3
1–403–291–2022 or 1–800–661–1645

3131–1 Ave. S, Lethbridge, AB T1J 4H1
1–403–329–9266 or 1–800–773–3962

Horticultural Societies
The Alberta Horticultural Association
email: apittao@telusplanet.net

The Calgary Horticultural Society
1–403–287–3469 www.calhort.org/

The Clearwater Garden Club
(Rocky Mountain House)
email: prowler@telusplanet.net

Country Gardens Garden Club
(Strathmore)
email: countrygardens@shaw.ca

The Edmonton Horticultural Society
email: donna@icangarden.com

The Dawson Creek and District Horticultural Society
email: CreditValleyHort@yahoo.com
(Contact: Dorothy Fast)

Drumheller Valley Garden Club
email: flwrabby@telusplanet.net

Grande Prairie Garden Club
email: gpgardeners@yahoo.ca
www.geocities.com/gpgardeners/
gpgardenclub.html

The Growing Pains Horticulture Club
email: sage2@telusplanet.net

Jisper Garden Club (Edson)
email: gardipee@telusplanet.net
or cbissell@telusplanet.net

Lacombe and District Garden Club
1–403–885–2062 (Contact: Beverly Atkins)

Lethbridge and District Horticultural Society email: pearsond@em.agr.ca

Lloydminster Horticultural Society
email: apittao@bordercity.com
www.lloydminster.org/hort/

Lobstick Garden Lovers Garden Club
email: dianesch@telusplanet.net

Medicine Hat Horticultural Society
1–403–527–2792
(Contact: Anne Burnhardt)

Morinville Garden Club
email: rlkampen@shaw.ca
www.telusplanet.net/public/pietrzyk/mgc/

Pembina Garden Club (Westlock/Dapp region) email: dlbaker@oanet.com

Petals Garden Club (Okotoks)
email: debbielp@telusplanet.net

Red Deer and District Garden Club
email: rdgc@shaw.ca
www.members.shaw.ca/rdgc/
home.htm

Rolling Hills Gardening Club (Brooks)
1–403–964–2003

St. Albert and District Garden Club
email: dharriso@telusplanet.net

Stony Plain Horticultural Society
email: sbmckay@telusplanet.net

Tofield Garden Club
email: pigchip@telusplanet.net

Gardens to Visit
The Cascade of Time Gardens
Administration Building, Banff, AB
www.beenthereseenthat.com/ab/
albertapages/pg02.htm
www.parkscanada.pch.gc.ca/banff/
1–403–762–1550

Boreal Botanic Garden
Box 1106, High Level, AB T0H 1Z0

Brewery Gardens
Off 1st Ave. S and Brewery Hill in
Lethbridge, AB
1–403–320–4097

*Calgary Zoo, Botanical Garden and
Prehistoric Park*
1300 Zoo Road NE,
Calgary, AB T2E 7V6
www.calgaryzoo.ab.ca/
1–800–588–9993, 1–403–232–9300

Devonian Botanic Garden
On Hwy. 60, 5 km N of Devon, AB
www.discoveredmonton.com/
devonian/ 1–780–987–3054

George Pegg Botanic Garden
On Hwy. 43, 2 km N of Glenevis, AB
Box 82, Glenevis, AB T0E 0X0
1–780–785–2421

Muttart Conservatory
9626–96A St., Edmonton, AB
T6C 4L8
www.gov.edmonton.ab.ca/comm_
services/city_op_attractions/muttart/
email: monica.lobb@gov.edmonton.ab.ca
1–780–496–8735

Nikka Yuko Centennial Garden
Mayor Magrath Drive and 8 Ave. S next
to Henderson Lake
Box 751, Lethbridge, AB T1J 3Z6
www.japanesegarden.ab.ca
1–403–328–3511

*Olds College Arboretum and Botanical
Gardens*
4500–50 St., Olds, AB T4H 1R6
www.oldscollege.ab.ca
email: dherbert@admin.oldscollege.ab.ca
1–800–661–6537, 1–403–556–8371

Rundle Wood Gardens
1643 Altadore Ave. SW, Calgary, AB T2T
2P8
www.telusplanet.net/public/rundlegd/ind
ex.html
email: info@rundlewoodgardens.ab.ca
1–403–243–9982

Trochu Arboretum and Gardens
North Road at the N end of Trochu, AB
www.albertasouth.com/town/trochu.html
1–403–442–4369, 1–403–442–3792

ACKNOWLEDGEMENTS

We all had a lot of fun working on this book. I would like to thank my fellow garden writers at Lone Pine, Don Williamson and Laura Peters, for their many contributions and discussions on the merits of composting, mulching and turfgrass versus xeriscapes. We were joined in our gardening discussions by Heather Markham and Nancy Foulds, who provided support and inspiration. We would also like to thank photographers Tamara Eder and Tim Matheson.

We are grateful for the many people who opened their gardens for us to photograph, both in Alberta and elsewhere. Thanks go to Alberta gardeners Tony and Milton Castelino, Ernst and Tamara Eder, Gerry Forestier, Trevor and Cherylynne Horbachewsky, Anita Jenkins, Lesley Knight, Bill Kozak, Heather Markham, Alex Rosato and Jeff Ross. As well we'd like to thank the Devonian Botanic Garden, Greenland Garden Centre, La Boheme Restaurant, Laurel's Flower & Garden and the Muttart Conservatory (Alberta); Adamson's Heritage Nursery Ltd., Select Roses and VanDusen Botanical Garden (British Columbia); Barbara and Douglas Bloom, Thea and Don Bloomquist and Cranbrook Gardens (Michigan); and the International Rose Test Garden (Oregon) for kindly allowing us to photograph their plants and gardens.

We would also like to thank the Lone Pine staff: Shane Kennedy, Nancy Foulds, editors Sandra Bit and Lee Craig and designer and Master Gardener Heather Markham. The assistance of Jennifer Fafard and Carol Woo was also appreciated. Thanks also to Gerry Dotto for his work on the cover design and to Ian Sheldon for the lovely corner flourishes that grace the pages. Others helped in various ways, close-cropping photos and providing stylistic solutions, and we thank them as well.

Cover page photos:
January–spruce bough; February–crabapple branches; March–forsythia blossoms; April–primroses and tulips; May–lilac flower; June–hosta; July–shrub rose 'The Fairy'; August–dahlias; September–viburnum (highbush cranberry); October–pumpkins; November–hoarfrost at sunset; December–poinsettias